Finding Pat O'Brien

by

Kevin McNulty, Sr.
&
Marcia Tedford

Copyright © 2014 KMC PUBLISHING COMPANY
All rights reserved.
ISBN-10: 0989796523
ISBN-13: 978-0-9897965-21
(4th Edition, July, 2016)

DEDICATION

To Mayor Rex Rowe, Mayor of Momence - 1963-1989,
for his service to our country and his life of persistence

PHOTOGRAPH OF BEARER.

SIGNATURE OF BEARER.

Pat Alva O'Brien

TABLE OF CONTENTS

Part I **Lineage & Land** (Chapters 1-7 in "Lt. Pat O'Brien") **Page 21**

Summary   Martin O'Brien arrives in America, finding his way to Momence, Illinois, a town at the edge of the great Kankakee Marsh. He marries three times and is father or step-father to over twenty-five children. His boy Daniel is the last of his sons to come home from the Civil War. Daniel marries Margaret "Maggie" Hathaway who has recently moved to Momence from Indiana. Two of Margaret's sisters marry the Hansen boys and the close-knit O'Briens, Hathaways and Hansens form an extended family known to all in Momence.

Part II **Growing up Fearless** (Chapters 8-13 in "Lt. Pat O'Brien") **Page 39**

Summary   Daniel and Margaret O'Brien have a uniquely energetic boy named Alva who is called "Pat" from an early age. The first fifteen years of his life are full of daring adventure, found only in a frontier town as disparate as Momence. His natural charisma and charm captivate all those who know him and he possesses a total fascination for all things new. Today, much of Momence look the same as it did in Pat's day, refurbished and maintained by the proud people of this town.

Part III **Flying Machines** (Chapters 14-21 in "Lt. Pat O'Brien") **Page 49**

Summary   A generation of young zealots, including Pat O'Brien, looks skyward, as the new "American Century" begins. Pat first learns of the Wright Brothers in the newspaper. But he is sent to live with Margaret's sisters in Wyoming following the death of Daniel O'Brien and Perry Hathaway. On impulse, Pat leaves one day to attend the International Aviation Meet in Chicago, then spends the next year in flight school at West Pullman. One year later he is in California working for the Santa Fe Railroad where he meets the love of his life, Agnes MacMillan. But by 1916, with the war raging in Europe, he joins the Army Signal Corps at North Island in San Diego hoping to fly. Impatient with the pace of American involvement, he joins the newly formed Canadian flying group and heads for England and the war in Europe as an officer in the Royal Flying Corps.

Part IV **Sudden Folly** (Chapters 22-25 in "Lt. Pat O'Brien") **Page 63**

Summary   After intense battle training in England, Pat and Paul Raney finally head to France and the staging area for battle with Germany. On August 17 he is shot from the sky but survives. During recovery he watches from his field hospital wheelchair as his close friend Paul Raney is shot down and dies.

Part V **Determined Break** (Chapters 26-32 in "Lt. Pat O'Brien") **Page 79**

Summary   Pat is held prisoner by the Hun at the prison in Courtrai, Belgium. On September 8 he is being transferred to Germany's interior but leaps from a moving prison train and escapes. He then walks 72 days, over 250 miles to the Holland border and freedom, where he eventually makes it back to London and is welcomed by the King George of England in Buckingham Palace.

Part VI	**Home Again** (Chapters 33-38 in "Lt. Pat O'Brien")	**Page 89**

Summary Pat spends two months recovering in London then arrives back home in Momence. He is welcomed by nearly the entire town and celebrations go on for three days. It is the biggest thing to ever happen in this small town. After a week at home, Pat travels to every major city in the United States speaking in the largest venues in each town. His fame makes him a household name.

Part VII	**Elusive Journey** (Chapters 39-48 in "Lt. Pat O'Brien")	**Page 103**

Summary Pat visits Agnes MacMillan and they draw as close as ever. He gives her a ring but after trying unsuccessfully to rejoin the war, he chooses to travel to Siberia where the end of the war has not yet arrived for the Russians. Unknown to Pat, Agnes has had his child while he was gone to Europe. She doesn't tell him but asks about marriage. He asks her to wait and then is gone for five months.

Part VIII	**Downward Spiral** (Chapters 49-53 in "Lt. Pat O'Brien")	**Page 127**

Summary Pat returns to the United States and Agnes will not see him. He knows their relationship is over. He pours himself into business ventures including public relations work for his old friend John McGraw, manager of the New York Giants Baseball team. Unfortunately, McGraw is tied to mob figure Albert Rothstein and Pat finds the crowd uncomfortable. He meets Virginia Dale in Washington and marries her in two weeks. They move to California where he is to shoot a silent film.

Part IX	**Final Days** (Chapters 54-54 in "Lt. Pat O'Brien)	**Page 155**

Summary Pat's marriage begins to fail, business ventures are failing him and Sarah Ottis has moved in him and his wife. He follows his wife to the Hamilton Hotel one night after a fight. He attempts reconciliation with Virginia but is not successful. Later that evening he is found dead with a bullet through his head.

Part X	**Legacy** (Epilogue in "Lt. Pat O'Brien" plus new material)	**Page 185**

Summary Momence welcomes home the body of their hometown hero. Over 200 vehicles form the largest procession ever in the town. He is buried with no marker until years later in 2007 when citizens of Momence dedicate a military marker to his name.

Part XI	**Carol** (Newly discovered history)	**Page 207**

Summary The life of Carol (O'Brien) Hughes Floto is highlighted. Carol is the child born to Pat O'Brien and Agnes MacMillan. The likeness to Pat is striking. Photos and information is provided by Pat's blood grandchildren in a meeting with Kevin McNulty in 2014.

How to use this book

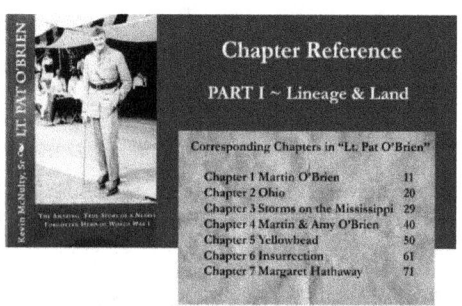

"Finding Pat O'Brien" is the companion book to **"Lt. Pat O'Brien,"** a novel by Kevin McNulty, Sr. about the life of Pat O'Brien.

This book provides the significant evidence gathered by Kevin McNulty, Sr. and Marcia Tedford over an eight-year period about the life of O'Brien. At the beginning of each part you will see a reference to the chapters in **"Lt. Pat O'Brien"** that correspond to the material in this book. The icon above appears with this information at the beginning of each part.

A full bibliography, periodical list and web reference section will appear in the next edition of this publication. The authors believe you are best to read the novel then refer back to this publication. But the *Lt. Pat O'Brien* synopsis included in this publication provides a good overview, as well. Those who have already read "Lt. Pat O'Brien" will find the information contained in this publication to be very enhancing to the novel.

ACKNOWLEDGEMENTS

Marcia Tedford

Neither this book, nor the novel *"Lt. Pat O'Brien,"* published in 2013, would have been written without Marcia Tedford. Marcia dedicated a number of years to finding Pat O'Brien, searching internet sites, talking to O'Brien family members and communicating with John Grech, Researcher and Historian for the 66th Squadron, Royal Flying Corps in England, prior to my involvement. Through the efforts of many Momence residents, our past mayor Rex Rowe, and Marcia, the family and community held a formal memorial service for Pat and placed a marker on his grave in 2007, eighty-seven years after he was buried in Momence.

Marcia's perseverance and passion to find Pat and tell his story was passed on to this author in 2007. For eight years, Marcia and I spent hours looking for Pat through countless emails, conversations, first-hand visits to places Pat had been, meetings with family members, extensive analysis of documents, translations of foreign evidence, inquiries sent to military and government archivists, and hours on the phone discussing, debating and fine-tuning the evidence.

Many times documents, newspaper reports and even quotes from those present in Pat's day conflicted. Indeed, the three Los Angeles newspaper reporters who covered Pat's death all told a different story. In every case, however, we dug until we could find a third or fourth piece of evidence that verified the truth. We felt we owed it to Pat to tell his story as accurately as we could from this distance. In the light of Pat's astonishing determination his whole life, we could hardly declare our efforts "good enough," at any point and we never did. It's our belief that more evidence about Pat's life will continue to come forward as more people learn about his life.

Once the writing of "Lt. Pat O'Brien" ensued, Marcia was the rudder who kept our creative ship on course. It was my charge to build a story based on all we had found. More than once, segments were redone and even whole chapters cut, combined or rewritten as evidence came forth. No greater example of this occurred than when, four years into our project, we received a call from Leslie Jacobs of Fallon, Nevada. "I am the illegitimate granddaughter of Pat O'Brien," were her stunning words. From Leslie and her sister Lori Floto of Reno, we learned about their mother who was born to Agnes MacMillan and Pat O'Brien in 1919.

Working on Pat O'Brien's story has been a "labor of love," for Marcia and me. We hope that more is discovered about this great American hero in the future. But without the initial efforts of Marcia Tedford, little of Pat O'Brien's story would be known to future generations.

WE THANK

Rex Rowe, Jean Stetson, Leslie Jacobs, Lori Floto, Ralph Cooper, Larry O'Brien, Gerald and Marggie Petro, Carla Petro Smith, Judy Hoffman, Elaine O'Brien Saindon, Robert Widener, Virginia Diane Fontaine, Francis Fontaine, Les Laskey, Michelle Chaney, Vic Johnson, Mike Jenkins, Gary Carruthers, James Chen, Lowell Library, Kankakee Library, Edward Chipman Library, Newton County Indiana Recorder of Deeds, Smithsonian National Air and Space Museum.

PREFACE

"Finding Pat O'Brien" is the companion book to the novel *"Lt. Pat O'Brien,"* by Kevin McNulty, Sr., Copyright © 2013, KMC Publishing Company. *"Finding Pat O'Brien"* has been written to document the most critical evidence uncovered by Kevin McNulty, Sr. and Marcia Tedford about the life of Alva F. "Pat" O'Brien.

Since the death of Pat O'Brien in 1920, his legacy and the facts of his life have been passed down via oral tradition through the O'Brien family and other residents of Momence. Naturally, much of the information was lost, changed, understated or embellished over the years. The goal of the authors has been to uncover documents and factual evidence in order to substantiate the facts of Pat's legacy. Both McNulty and Tedford would agree that, as a result of their six-plus years of research, Pat O'Brien's accomplishments, character and legacy have only been enhanced. What first appeared to be yet another "local hero" story has revealed itself to be much larger than even the most fantastic stories told over the years about Pat.

More is known about Pat O'Brien today than any time since his death. Until *"Lt. Pat O'Brien"* and this publication, few knew of the extent of Pat's speaking engagements, his travel through the world including Siberia and China, the actual route taken by Pat to escape Germany, the extensive newspaper coverage of his capture, escape, subsequent book tour or the details of his military career including flight record, honors and status within the military. Conversely, eight years of research have created as many new questions about Pat as answers to old questions. He was and is, today, an enigma.

Pat O'Brien was a simple small town kid and a fearless world traveler. He was a man of action yet reflective and intelligent. He was a humble patriot and a promotional showman at the same time. He could be methodical and systematic yet unconventional and daring. He was a visionary who also understood the restraints of his present condition. He was genuine, sincere and at the same time could be whimsical and elusive. His rugged individual victory against huge odds penetrated the American psyche and represented their spirit. He fit the American archetype of "one man against all odds." In addition, he did it all with that infectious smile earning him the nickname, "Smiling Pat."

In reality, the writing of *"Lt. Pat O'Brien,"* was finished at the end of four years. But an unanticipated phone call from a woman in Nevada opened up some startling new information about Pat O'Brien not known to anyone, including the O'Brien family in Momence. With the words, "I am the illegitimate granddaughter of Pat O'Brien," Leslie Jacobs, daughter of the child born out of wedlock to Pat O'Brien and Agnes MacMillan, added a new and, frankly, capstone chapter to Pat's life story.

Leslie and her sister Lori Floto had become interested in finding out more about their grandfather. They both knew Agnes as "Aunt Agnes" and possessed some astoundingly new information about her and her relationship with Pat. They contacted the Momence Chamber of Commerce after hearing someone was writing a book about Pat. Marcia Tedford had posted a note on the official Royal Flyer Corps' 66th Squadron historical website operated by the squadron's historian John Gretch. Eventually Leslie reached Marcia and Kevin with the news.

As part of the research for this book, McNulty traveled to Reno, Nevada on July 22-23, 2014 and met Leslie and Lori for the first time. Their stories and photos have become a significant part of Pat's story and are presented, for the first time, in this publication.

Clearly, the most frequent discussion about Pat O'Brien has always been the nature of his death. Was he murdered or did he commit suicide? O'Brian family members, known to the authors for years and interviewed for this project, have, to a person, always denied that Pat caused his own death. Beyond the contentions of the family, the most baffling reality that contradicts the suicide theory is how Pat lived his life. Was it not Pat himself who wrote of the "folly of despair" in his crisp and startling book *"Outwitting the Hun?"*

While no conclusion about Pat's death has been drawn in this book or *"Lt. Pat O'Brien"*, McNulty brings forth the involvement of Sarah Ottis and Pat's wife Virginia Dale in Pat's final days. Additionally, research into the three local newspaper stories covering Pat's death revealed three different reports on the location of the gunshot wound. The reader is also cautioned not to assume that present day standards for death investigations existed in 1920, for they did not. Modern forensics did not exist in 1920 and, in the case of Pat's death the scene was inspected twice by common detectives who relied extensively on their own personal observations and little science.

In addition, evidence indicates that Pat's estate all but disappeared despite efforts of his brother to "find Pat's money" following his death. Pat's sister Clara Clegg, who was in Los Angeles at the time of his death, escorted his body home, and was arguably Pat's closest sibling. She died penniless in the Solders' and Sailors' Home in Wilmington, Illinois, in 1943. Margaret's letter to the Air Force Association of Canada in 1925 also pointed to the families difficult times following Pat's death. In her letter she asked about the "whereabouts of my son," but speculation is that she was asking if Pat might have any further military pension.

Still there is no doubt that the savvy, steady and determined Pat O'Brien waned during the last year of his life, most notably as evidenced by his marriage to Virginia, who he had only known for three weeks before marrying her in Havana. And what straight-thinking man would have allowed a non-relative such as Sarah Ottis and her daughter live in his home alongside his wife?

While McNulty and Tedford would prefer to know that Pat did *not* end his own life, they took an honest and empirical approach to uncover facts and evidence that could lead the reader to one conclusion or another. Indeed, the authors went back and forth on the question throughout the project and to this day cannot say equivocally either way. Each holds a somewhat varied view of the matter based on known evidence. If and until further evidence comes forward, the nature of Pat's death will likely be debated for all time.

A number of significant Momence citizens saw fit to finally place a marker on the grave of Pat O'Brien in 2007. A big part of that effort came from the inspiration of Mayor Rex Rowe of Momence to whom this book is dedicated. Had this event not occurred, the impetus to research and document Pat O'Brien's life may have died with the final generation of Momence residents who knew of his legend. Fortunately for all of us, his story lives today and, hopefully, will be revealed further by future curious admirers, inspired to find Pat O'Brien.

SYNOPSIS

"Lt. Pat O'Brien," by Kevin McNulty, Sr.
KMC PUBLISHING COMPANY, Copyright 2013

Most small towns on the Illinois Prairie are products of agriculture. Even today, a drive from Chicago in the north to the southern forests of Shawnee, reveals one large grain elevator complex after another. The elevators are surrounded by main streets, comfortable homes with well-kept lawns and children riding bikes through familiar and safe surroundings. Other than the handful of towns near lakes, rivers or coal mines, most serve as collection centers for the fertile fields of Illinois.

While the small town of Momence, Illinois has certainly produced its share of bumper crops, the story of this town cannot be fully explained by agriculture alone. To its west, lay the open prairie but east of town was a marsh that extended ten miles to the Indiana line and beyond. It drained through the middle of town, extended west to the Illinois River and eventually the great Mississippi. Before the farmers arrived, the marsh was teeming with trappers. Just fifty miles south of the Chicago River and Fort Dearborn, Momence was a fur trading center before Chicago existed. French fur traders crossed the shallow portion of the Kankakee River at Momence, pausing to do business with the local scavengers of the marsh and downing some whiskey before heading on to trading posts north.

River folks from Tennessee and Kentucky, French Canadian furriers, European farmers and a large contingent of merchants, bankers and craftsmen from the east all descended on this melting pot prior to 1900. Like all towns within a day's ride of Chicago, Momence also had its share of railroads following the Civil War.

In 1834, Martin O'Brien arrived at Momence from Ireland after two years of travel from New York to New Orleans to Ohio and, finally, Illinois by foot, steamship and horseback. Before his three sons were old enough to fight in "Abe Lincoln's war," Martin left his family for California, chasing gold before returning home, broke. He witnessed his boys' return from war and start of their own families. He died before his son Daniel's wife Margaret Hathaway brought forth Alva F. "Pat" O'Brien, born in 1890. Had Martin known young Pat, he would have seen the obvious similarity to himself. Pat O'Brien was a boy full of energy. He was curious about everything and his tenacity was evident at an early age. He also had a charm that disarmed even the most forbidding adult.

Pat lost his father at age eleven. Having little interest in formal schooling, he lived a "Huck Finn" existence playing hooky from school and in the summer, leading a pack of loyal tenderfoots who hung on his every word. Young Pat grew up amid blacksmith shops, trapper camps, lumber mills, farms, tanneries, doily covered eateries, taverns and a bountiful river full of fish.

But by the time Pat hit his early teens, Momence was changing. The Wennerholm Livery went from shoeing horses to repairing combustible engines. The streets in town were being upgraded from dusty ruts to smooth brick. The first automobile appeared in town and one week before Pat's thirteenth birthday Orville and Wilbur Wright flew their winged plane for twelve seconds at Kitty Hawk. Stories began to fill the newspaper that man may actually learn to fly. Pat was thrilled by it all. He began jumping on trains, heading north to discover all that was not possible in his hometown. Chicago, which totaled four thousand people when Martin arrived in Momence, had one million residents by the time Pat was fourteen years old.

By age sixteen his father's military benefits ran out and Margaret sent Pat away to live with his aunts in Cody, Wyoming. With one foot in the nineteenth century and the other in the twentieth century, Pat set off to make it on his own. He worked odd jobs and was appreciative of his aunts and uncles but after nearly three years, he'd had his fill of Wyoming and wanted to return home. Even the presence of Wild Bill Cody, who Pat surely met, was not enough to hold him in the isolated west.

Pat's brother Elmer farmed in the San Joaquin Valley and it seemed logical for Pat join him, which he did until age 21. It was there that he first met Ed Hesser, one of the many amateur aeroplane enthusiasts building experimental aircraft in the Central Valley. Pat and Hesser built two crude aircraft during 1910 and early 1911 and it provided Pat his first "hands-on" experience with the practical application of aviation he had read so much about since his youth.

Pat's enthusiasm for flight increased dramatically during his time in California and in the summer of 1911, he returned home to attend the International Aviation Meet at Grant Park, downtown Chicago. The event was literally a "who's who" of flying mavericks. He was hooked. He decided to stay home and attend formal flight school at West Pullman near Chicago. He perfected his craft and discovered that he had all the instincts only top pilots possess.

After a year of training, Pat headed back to California, this time settling in the San Francisco area where he found a job with the Santa Fe Railroad at Richmond. Railroad jobs were plentiful and Pat felt "at home" riding trains. He found plenty of opportunities to offer his services as a test pilot and spent every free moment flying planes and working again with Hesser on projects.

By the spring of 1914, Pat had increased responsibility at the railroad and had put a good sum of money in the bank. He'd also met a significant airplane designer from Stockton named Joe Cato and spent nearly every weekend as his test pilot. Three events occurred that year that would set Pat on a different path. Pat attended the Panama Pacific Exposition at Presidio which featured a huge air show. The war exploded all over Europe in June. And he met Agnes MacMillan from San Francisco.

For the next two years, Pat and Agnes were together constantly joining their entourage of friends on weekends at picnics, parties and their favorite bar at the Ivy Inn. But by January of 1916, driven by his passion to fly, his patriotism to fight, and a restless nature, he announced to Agnes that he would be joining the army.

Pat O'Brien joined the U.S. Army Signal Corps in 1916 at age 26. He knew that the future of flying would be in the military and the Signal Corps was charged with testing the feasibility of aircraft as weapons. The testing was at North Island in San Diego and Pat was among the very first Army Signal Corps assigned to test the Army's newly acquired machine. But as enthusiastic as Pat was about military aviation, the U.S. Army seemed to be dragging their feet. Six months into his service, he resigned from the Signal Corps and joined the newly formed Canadian Air Corps.

The British had charged Canada with generating thousands of pilots. The Royal Air Force had been butchered by the Germans in the past year. Pat knew he'd be on the "fast track" if he joined the Canadians. After saying goodbye to Agnes and his friends in Richmond he reported to Toronto and was among the first pilots to qualify for Europe. It was at Camp Borden in Toronto where he met his best buddy Paul Raney.

The two roommates trained hard and by July of 1917, following a quick visit to Momence, Pat and the others sailed for England and the war. Additional training in England taught both men about military aviation and within weeks, Pat and Paul were flying missions over Germany from the Pilot's Pool in France. On August 17, Pat O'Brien was shot from the sky 8,000 feet above Germany. The bullet entered his upper lip, passed out the bottom of his mouth and lodged in his throat.

Pat was operated on in a shanty field hospital by German doctors who treated him with disdain. Days later, while recovering, he sat in the sun with other patients and witnessed the killing of his best friend Paul Raney in a dogfight overhead. When he asked a guard to verify the identity of the downed pilots, the German guard brought him a photo found on one of the bodies. It was a photo of Pat and Paul on board ship from Canada. He knew he had lost his friend.

Pat spent three weeks in prison at Courtrai, which featured humiliating prisoners in parades through town, lice infestation, and "entertainment" for the German guards involving hungry dogs attacking helpless prisoners in the prison yard. Scuttlebutt around prison was that Pat and his fellow officers would be transferred deep into Germany. The humiliating and acute conditions of Pat's captivity thus far convinced him that he was better off trying to escape then spending the rest of the war in prison. Pat developed a strong dislike for the Kaiser and the German Army as a result of Courtrai.

On September 9, Pat and a group of other officers were on a train for the interior of Germany. They were to be brought to a reprisal camp designed to store German armaments amid prisoners of war, so as to avoid bombings. About thirty minutes into the trip, wrestling with his decision until the final moment, Pat stood up, grabbed the luggage rack and lifted himself out of the open window, feet first. His wounds reopened, he was temporarily knocked out but as the train's brakes squealed in the night, Pat gathered his wits and ran deep into the woods. He ran until he could no longer hear the guards or their dogs.

What followed was a 72 day, 250-mile walk in a northern direction through Germany, Luxemburg and Belgium to the Holland border. Pat walked by night and slept during the day. He swam dozens of rivers and canals, particularly in Belgium, nearly drowning when swimming the Meuse River. He gradually stole enough clothes to replace his British uniform. He ventured undercover into small towns on occasion to find food but, for the most part, he lived on turnips and berries found along the way. He had some harrowing confrontations with German soldiers in cities where he played mute. In the countryside he hid in the woods. But eventually he made it to the Holland border.

Against all odds, he escaped. His final feat involved traversing a nine foot electrified fence at the Holland border within eyesight of German sentries. He arrived in London a few days later, looking nothing like a British officer. Once he convinced officials that he was an escaped prisoner, he found himself, one week later, in a private audience with King George at Buckingham Palace. The King and all of Britain were astounded at his escape.

Word spread throughout Britain and the United States about his fantastic feat. Newspapers all over the United States flashed front page stories about the Irish-American lad from the small Illinois town of Momence who had achieved the impossible. Pat's legacy began immediately and during his first few weeks in London, he spoke before a number of military audiences who hung on his every word. It was at this time that reporters recognized his uncanny ability to stir large audiences.

Naturally, since the war was still on, he could not tell his whole story but before he arrived home, Pat wrote a book entitled *"Outwitting the Hun"* about his escape. He was contracted with Lee Keedick, a New York promoter, for an extensive book tour in the U.S. In 1918, he would become the top public speaker in the United States, surpassing William Jennings Bryan. He spoke in every major venue in the U.S. and spoke in dozens of theaters in small towns across the country.

Pat O'Brien returned home to Momence on January 7, 1918. Less than two weeks later, after a grand reception, a speech in Momence and numerous appearances around Kankakee County and Chicago, he spoke at Carnegie Hall in New York before a full house. Word of his story exploded across the American press. In addition to getting paid well for his speeches, his book sales soared and he became quite well off, financially.

Eventually, the luster of the war hero began to fade. Pat had already spoken in every major venue in the country. His final appearances included twenty-minute Vaudeville shows in New York and other cities and Chautauqua tours in the Midwest. Pat understood that his speaking days were over. He also felt the tug of regret for not having given enough in the war. He had tried to rejoin the RAF but could not pass the physical test. He was turned down by the U.S. Army, the French Foreign Legion and the Lafayette Escadrille. More than anything else, he desired to return to fight once again.

His efforts to re-enter the war baffled Agnes. After all, Pat had given her a ring of engagement during the year, yet he talked about re-entering the service. Like so many survivors of war, Pat was haunted by the price paid by his fellow soldiers who never made it home, particularly Paul Raney. He felt he had not given enough.

When the war ended in November of 1918, Pat saw one last opportunity to serve by entering Siberia where Vladimir Lenin was still fighting with loyal Tsarist armies. Allied troops were attempting to escape the chaos along the Trans-Siberian Railroad. Pat felt that with his railroad experience and his cunning abilities to escape the enemy, he could be of help. He went to Vladivostok via Japan and China and traveled west toward Moscow before abandoning his trip on the famous railroad as Red forces began to move east. Pat headed straight south into Mongolia and China by various means returning home at the Seattle Port on October 26, 1919.

Before he'd left for Russia, he and Agnes met for the last time. Unknown to Pat was the birth of Agnes' baby Carol, who was only a few months old. Agnes pressed Pat regarding marriage and chose not to tell Pat of the child. He requested "one more trip" to Russia which indicated to Agnes that he would likely never settle down. At that point, she made a decision to give up her child for adoption and Pat never knew of baby Carol. Upon returning from Russia, Pat blindly tried to make contact with Agnes. After a number calls that did not get through and interceptions by Agnes' close friend Arlene, Pat finally reached Agnes by phone from Chicago. It was obvious that Agnes had moved on and Pat had lost her.

Pat returned home to Momence. He also began spending some of his money. He invested in an auto sales company in Southern California and purchased a farm in Indiana which his brother worked. He was hounded by many individuals with an equal number of sound and frivolous investment schemes. With his war years behind him and no serious need for money, Pat considered his options. He traveled to New York to see his old promoter Keedick. While it was evident that Pat's speaking days were over, Lee had a contact interested in Pat for a silent picture. Pat's old friend Hesser, now a known photographer in Los Angeles, would arrange a meeting with the producers.

Before beginning work on the film *"Shadows of the West,"* Pat made a few speeches along the east coast. With the end of the war, military recruiting diminished drastically. Retired military officers and men who served with distinction were regularly called upon to speak before recruits and newly enlisted men. At one event in Washington DC, Pat found himself on a panel with Eddie Rickenbacker who was still in service and Canada's flying ace William "Billie" Bishop. Overseeing a portion of the event was a 2nd Lieutenant named Hugh Livingston. Hugh and his sister Virginia were both from a well-to-do family in Washington DC. Virginia was a reporter and aspiring actress though she had yet to have any major film roles.

Hugh Livingston drove Pat to the panel presentation. He had agreed to let his sister Virginia ride along to get an exclusive interview with the war hero. Still distraught by his break up with Agnes, Pat was swept up by the personality and beauty of Virginia Dale. Dale was her acting name. At the event, a second woman, who would play a significant role in Pat's life, was also present. Sarah Ottis was the estranged wife of Lieutenant Colonel Daniel Mortimer Ottis of Springfield, Illinois. The Colonel had been one of General Pershing's medical officers during the war. Ever since the divorce, Sarah became part of the social scene in Washington on her ex-husband's name and was serving as a host for the panel event. She had met Pat O'Brien before. In fact, she was present at his first major speech at Orchestra Hall in Chicago two weeks after Pat returned from London. Virginia and Sarah met each other at the speech and quickly became regular acquaintances. Once Virginia learned of Pat's upcoming film shoot, she plotted to tie her chances to the famous O'Brien and perhaps earn the film role she had yet to acquire.

During Pat's time in New York he was seen with some of the more famous people of the day. A number of famous businessmen, sports and entertainment people liked being seen with the war hero and Pat enjoyed their company, too. Hesser knew many of the entertainment folks due to his growing career as a celebrity photographer. Pat became good friends with John J. McGraw, manager of the New York Giants baseball team and a partner with Arnold "The Brain" Rothstein who was dean of the Jewish mob in New York. McGraw and Rothstein were introducing gambling, horseracing and luxury hotels to Havana, Cuba, the playground for rich and famous after the war. The grand opening strategy was to get as many rich and famous people in Havana as possible. McGraw convinced Pat to come to Cuba.

By the time the Havana week occurred, Sarah Ottis had worked an arrangement to not only invite herself but convinced Virginia to attend. Sarah worked behind the scenes to schedule Pat's first meeting with film producers in Havana, as well. It was the beginning of a whirlwind invasion of Pat's business, his privacy and his money. Pat made his share of mistakes. On New Year's Day 1920, obviously not thinking with the cool head that brought him to freedom during the war, he married Virginia Dale in Havana, three weeks after meeting her for the first time.

The film went forward but not without problems. The government banned the first release due to its inflammatory affront to the newly perceived enemy of the United States, the Japanese. Sarah, her daughter Gwen and Virginia eventually all lived in Pat's new Los Angeles home and as 1920 came to a close, the marriage and Pat's bank account were in serious jeopardy. Following a serious fight over money one night Virginia, encouraged by Sarah, left the house for the Alexandria Hotel. Distraught and convinced he could save his marriage, Pat threw Sarah out of the house and got a room at the hotel to make amends to his wife. In the very early morning of December 18, 1920, a young clerk entered room 613 to investigate a loud noise. When he opened the door, he saw Pat sitting in a large chair, holding a pistol in his hand with a bullet through his head. He was dead at age 30.

Part I

Lineage & Land

Chapter Reference

PART I ~ Lineage & Land

Corresponding Chapters in "Lt. Pat O'Brien"

Chapter 1 Martin O'Brien	11
Chapter 2 Ohio	20
Chapter 3 Storms on the Mississippi	29
Chapter 4 Martin & Amy O'Brien	40
Chapter 5 Yellowhead	50
Chapter 6 Insurrection	61
Chapter 7 Margaret Hathaway	71

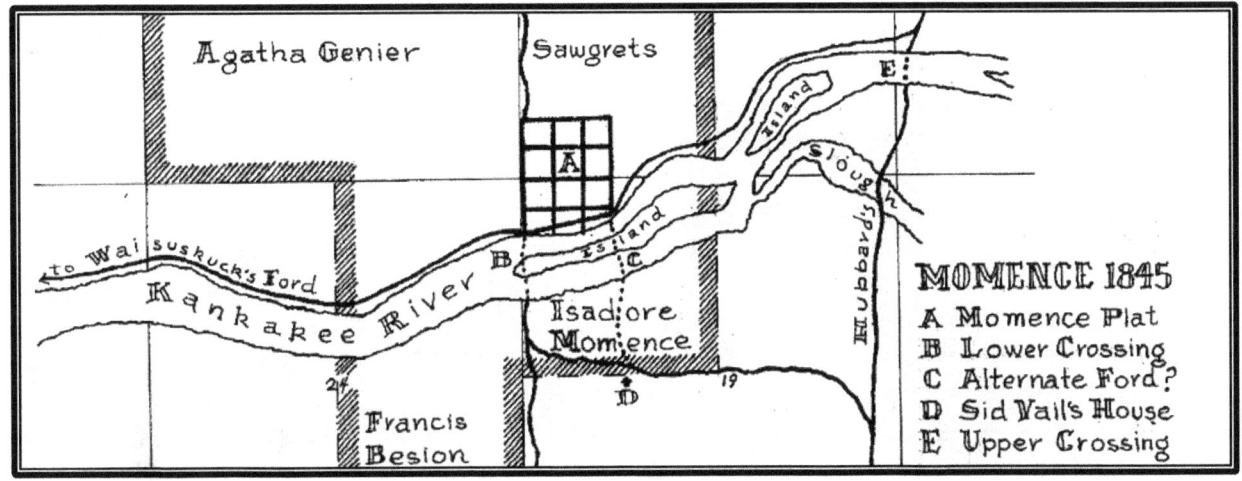

PART I - LINEAGE & LAND ~ In the 1800's, two Irish families, the Hathaways and the O'Briens, settled on land fifty miles south of Lake Michigan in Illinois, near the Kankakee River. The O'Briens arrived when Martin O'Brien purchased land along Vincennes Trail in 1832. O'Brien outlived his first wife Amy who died in 1848. He married Sarah Ruggles in 1849 and took a third wife by the name of Louisa in 1860, last name unknown. As a result, Martin was father or step-father to twenty five children. Perry Hathaway arrived in Momence in 1883 from Indiana with his wife Mary Elizabeth Drake. The Hathaways had six children. Their families merged in 1872 when Daniel O'Brien, born to Martin and Amy, took the hand of Margaret Hathaway, Perry and Mary Elizabeth's oldest girl. The two were married in Kankakee, Illinois in 1872.

Prior to the formal organization of the Illinois Territory in 1809, fur trade flourished along the great "highways" of primitive travel. Illinois was at the confluence of the Mississippi, Missouri, Ohio and Illinois Rivers and the tactical "capillary exchange" of pelts from trapper to trader occurred at points along smaller tributaries such as the Iroquois, Sangamon and Kankakee rivers. The "crossing," at what would become Momence, attracted traders heading north as did the marshland to the east, a trapper's paradise. By 1830, most of the Indians had been "relocated" west of the Mississippi and a wave of European immigrants began to claim acres of cheap land north, south and west of town. Momence was incorporated in 1834 - Chicago not until in 1837, making Momence the oldest community in northeastern Illinois.

At the turn of the century, The Industrial Revolution would take deep swaths of human energy and grit from this place, as evidenced in the life of its favorite son, Pat O'Brien.

Momence during its late frontier days. This photo was used as the inspiration to the opening chapter in *"Lt. Pat O'Brien."* It shows William Parrish in his wagon with daughter Carrie Marie in town "on errands." **Below:** Front Street looking northwest. On the day Pat and his friends scampered off to swim the new-flooded quarry, "Lt. Pat O'Brien" depicts Pat running down this wooden sidewalk past Charles Astle's Hardware Store. During Pat's day's growing up, he could be seen all throughout town exploring the world as he knew it.

Within the same community lived aristocratic and educated merchants, bankers and businessmen from the East alongside the trappers of the marsh who settled the area first and stayed.

THE O'BRIENS (from Martin)

MARTIN OBRIEN
Born 12/9/1810   Died 9/12/1876
Married   1st Wife   Amy Hurley 11/18/1834, Miami County, Ohio
            2nd Wife   Sarah Ruggles Hurley (Thomas) 8/15/1849
            3rd Wife   Louisa Cook Hurley (James) 1/16/1860

Martin was born in Ireland – Arrived in the U.S. 1830 via Quebec, Canada
Martin traveled throughout eastern and southern states for two years
Martin came to Momence in 1836 Buried in Nichols Cemetery near Momence

AMY HURLEY   [Martin's 1st Wife]
Born 1815   **Died** 1848
Married Martin O'Brien in 1834 in Miami County, Ohio
     Children by Martin
         James O'Brien (1838-1888)
         Baby O'Brien (1839-1839)
         Rhoda O'Brien (1840-1893)
         Baby O'Brien (1841-1841)
         Thomas O'Brien (Born 1842-Died 9-/9/1863)
            Thomas was killed serving in the Union Army
            Company "D" Forty-second Illinois Infantry
         Jefferson O'Brien (Born 11/13/1844 Died 3/16/1924)
            Married Lovisa Burns 4/15/1866
               Born   1/12/1847   Died 1946
               Born in Momence. Her father's name was
               Alva (same as Pat's)
               Children   Grace O'Brien Born 1868
                            Florence O'Brien Born 1873
            Jefferson born in Illinois (Yellowhead)
            Jefferson was 4 when his mother died. Went to live with
            Ansil Chipman of Grant Park until 1859 (14). Jefferson
            moved back with father for 2 years in 1859. Enlisted
            Company "D" Illinois Forty-second Infantry 8/71861

         Daniel O'Brien (Born 1/20/1846 Died 12/7/1901) [55]
            Married Margaret "Maggie" Hathaway O'Brien 9/9/1872
               Born 10/15/1853 Died 10/8/1930
            Enlisted 1-5-1864 / Discharged 1865 "Union Army
            Civil War company "K" 113th Vol. Infantry"
            Enlisted 1/5/1854
         Merwin O'Brien Seager
            Merwin adopted by Russell and Marilla (Hathaway) Seager
            of Grant Park. Married Lavin McKinstry.

SARAH RUGGLES HURLEY
Born 1816 (Adams Co. Ohio)   Died 1859)   **Martin's 2nd Wife**
Married Thomas Edward Hurley - (1792-1847)
    Children by Thomas
        Eliza Hurley (1834-1880)
        Daniel Hurley (1835-)
        Cornelius Hurley (1838)
        Sarah Hurley (1843)
        Mahala Hurley (1844-1880)
        James T. Hurley (1847)
Married Martin O'Brien in   8/15/1849
    Children by Martin
        Martin O'Brien (1811-1876)
        William L. O'Brien (1850-1926)

LOUISA UNKNOWN
Born 1816   **Died**   1880   **Martin's 3rd Wife**
Married James Hurley
    Children by James
        Zachariah C. (1842-1910
        Amanda (1842-1901)
        Meredith (1848-)
        Samuel (1851-)
        Emma (1853)
        George (1858-)
Married Martin O'Brien 1/16/1860
    Children by Martin
        Mulligan (1861)

THE UNITED STATES OF AMERICA,

CERTIFICATE No. 12,944

To all to whom these Presents shall come, Greeting:

WHEREAS Martin O'Bryne, of Will County, Illinois ha_ deposited in the GENERAL LAND OFFICE of the United States, a Certificate of the REGISTER OF THE LAND OFFICE at Chicago whereby it appears that full payment has been made by the said Martin O'Bryne, according to the provisions of the Act of Congress of the 24th of April, 1820, entitled "An act making further provision for the sale of the Public Lands," for the North West quarter of the South West quarter of Section thirty two, in Township thirty two, North, of Range fourteen, East, of the third Principal Meridean, in the District of Lands subject to sale at Chicago, Illinois, containing forty acres,

according to the official plat of the survey of the said Lands, returned to the General Land Office by the SURVEYOR GENERAL, which said tract ha_ been purchased by the said Martin O'Bryne.

NOW KNOW YE, That the United States of America, in consideration of the Premises, and in conformity with the several acts of Congress, in such case made and provided, HAVE GIVEN AND GRANTED, and by these presents DO GIVE AND GRANT, unto the said Martin O'Bryne, and to his heirs, the said tract above described: TO HAVE AND TO HOLD the same, together with all the rights, privileges, immunities, and appurtenances of whatsoever nature, thereunto belonging, unto the said Martin O'Bryne, and to his heirs and assigns forever.

In Testimony Whereof, I, James K. Polk PRESIDENT OF THE UNITED STATES OF AMERICA, have caused these Letters to be made PATENT, and the SEAL of the GENERAL LAND OFFICE to be hereunto affixed.

GIVEN under my hand, at the **CITY OF WASHINGTON,** the first day of May in the Year of our Lord one thousand eight hundred and forty five and of the **INDEPENDENCE OF THE UNITED STATES** the Sixty ninth.

BY THE PRESIDENT: James K. Polk

By J. Knox Walker Sec'y.

S. H. Laughlin RECORDER of the General Land Office.

Land Deed - Martin O'Brien - 1842

ORIGINS OF MOMENCE, ILLINOIS

From Thesis Memories of Momence Township 1776-1976
Elizabeth B. Morrison, 1976, University of Illinois

During the year 1822 Hubbard established a track, or trace as it was often called, from his post at Bunkum (present day Iroquois) south well beyond Danville and north to Chicago. The Indians with whom he traded were the Potawatomi, described by early French missionaries as hunters and fishers of war-like bearing living north of Lake Huron, then later along the coast of Lake Michigan. Early in the eighteenth century they had migrated to northern Indiana and northern Illinois. The men hunted and Fished, the women raised the crops: corn, beans, squash, and melons.

There were several of their villages in the Kankakee valley; Chief Yellowhead's village near Sherburnville, Wais-kuks near Waldron, She-mor-gar or Soldier's village, and the largest, Shawanasee's village at Rock Creek. These Potawatomi were excellent trappers, no longer war-like, but accustomed to the white man and his trade goods: guns, blankets, copper pots, clothing and whiskey. Although they had lived in the Kankakee valley just a little over one hundred years, it was indeed their wonderful land. Beaver Lake and the marshes eastward were natural fish hatcheries; waterfowl and food animals were plentiful and crops grew well. Yet they were persuaded to give it up.

President Jackson needed more frontier land for the pioneer families; he wanted the nation to grow westward. Since the Indians were in the way he requested Congress to pass an Indian Removal Act authorizing treaties with the Indians for their land, and resettling them on reservations west of the Mississippi. At Tippecanoe, Indiana, in 1832, the Potawatomi sold their lands in what is now Kankakee County to the United States government.

Certain choice land was reserved for chiefs or their families, principally in the area that is now Kankakee and Bourbonnais— reservations ranging from 320 to 3200 acres in size. However, these Indians chose to sell their reservation and go with their people to Iowa. The upheaval took place gradually, a few groups at a time. By 1838 almost all the Potawatomi had left their "wonderful land home".

Settlers came to Kankakee County in 1834, after the federal government signed the Treaty of Camp Tippecanoe in 1832. As word spread about the government acquiring the land, many immigrants of New York and Vermont moved their way west, mostly locating in Momence, Illinois.

An act of the Illinois Legislature created Kankakee County out of the north part of Iroquois County and the south part of Will County on February 11, 1853. The six original townships were: Yellowhead, Rockville, Bourbonnais, Momence, Aroma Park, and Limestone. The population of the new county was about 8,000. It wasn't until 1855 that the two western townships of Norton and Essex were taken from Vermilion County and added to Kankakee County.

First known as "Lower Crossing", Momence was named after a local Potawatomi, Isadore Moness. Momence was first platted by Dr. Hiram Todd in 1846.

THE HATHAWAYS (From Perry)

O.H.P. "PERRY" HATHAWAY
Born 1826 **Died** 1906 **[80]** (Momence Cemetery)
Married Mary Elizabeth Drake
Perry Hathaway was born in Shelby Country, Ohio on the grounds once occupied by Fort Jefferson (1791-1796).

MARY ELIZABETH DRAKE
Born 1829 **Died** 1906 **[77]**
Married Perry Hathaway
Mary died in Momence
    Children by Perry
        John Hathaway (Born ? - Died 1852) - Married Ida Unknown
        Margaret "Maggie" **(PAT'S MOTHER - see detail under Daniel)**
        Born 10/15/1853 Died 10/8/1930 **[77]** (Momence Cemetery)
        Arleta Cecilia (1859-1833) - Married Theodore Hansen (1857-1933)
        Jeremiah (9/3/1891 - 7/11/1889)
        Hattie Belle (1867-10/22/1926) - Married John Heinrich Hansen

Theodore Hansen and John Hansen were brothers and they married the O'Brien sisters Arleta Cecilia and Hattie Belle. They moved from Momence and settled in Wyoming. Pat's mother sent Pat to live with the Hansens when Daniel's war benefits ran out. Maggie could not afford to raise Pat. He left home fatherless at age 16 returned two years later to study flying in Chicago then headed for California.

MARGARET "MAGGIE" HATHAWAY O'BRIEN

Above: Daniel and Margaret's marriage certificate, 1872
Below: Baby Pat's earliest known photo. He was "Smiling Pat" from the start.

THE O'BRIENS (from Daniel & Margaret O'Brien)

DANIEL O'BRIEN
Born 1/20/1846 **Died** 12/07/1901 **[55]** (Momence Cemetery)
Married Margaret "Maggie" O'Brien 9/9/1872
Born in Yellowhead Township
Daniel died at home in Momence

PAT'S FATHER

MARGARET "MAGGIE" HATHAWAY O'BRIEN
Born 10/15/1853 **Died** 10/8/1930 **[77]** (Momence Cemetery)
Married Daniel O'Brien 9/9/1872
Came to Momence in 1872 with parents and siblings
Early in 1872 married Daniel later that year [19]
Born in Gates, Porter, County Near Valparaiso, Indiana
Died from "heart trouble which developed into dropsy."

PAT'S MOTHER

PAT'S SIBLINGS

PA Age at Pat's birth

PD Age at Pat's death

[ ] Age at death

LILA A. O'BRIEN
Born 4/17/1874 **Died** 4/1/1924 **[50]**
Married Benjamin Franklin Worley 2/14/1898
Born in Momence, Illinois
Suffered from rheumatism for years
Died in Lowell, Indiana

BENJAMIN FRANKLIN WORLEY   Lila's Husband
Born 1855   Died 1933
1st Wife Anna Sargent   Born   Died 1877
2nd Wife Lila O'Brien No children but took in her niece Miss Marie (O'Brien) Worley
Marie was Elmer's daughter (O'Brien)

CLARA B. O'BRIEN
Born 2/27/1876 **Died** 11/5/1943 **[57]**
Married Matthew Clegg 12/24/1892
Clara and Matthew lived in Momence.
Attended Pat's Funeral
Attended Margaret's Funeral
Clara died in Wilmington Soldier Widow's home, penniless

MATTHEW CLEGG   Clara's Husband
Born 9/21/1861 Died 2/18/1917 **[56]**
Married Clara B. O'Brien 12/24/1892
Moved from England to Australia as a young boy
He later moved to the U.S. in 1883
Highly trained as shoemaker.
Clegg owned a shoe store in Momence

ELMER E. O'BRIEN
Born 6/20/1878   **Died**
Married   1st Wife Lulu Ducharme (maiden name)
                2nd Wife Elizabeth Radtke
Attended Pat's funeral

LULU Ducharme O'BRIEN   **Elmer's 1st Wife**
Born   Died
Divorced Elmer and married Harry Laskey
Child - Marie O'Brien Worley born 1903 (Raised by Lila and Benjamin Worley)
Child - Elmer O'Brien - born 1902 (Went with Lulu and step-father)

ELIZABETH Radtke O'BRIEN   **Elmer's 2nd Wife**
Born   Died
Married Elmer   1/05/1921 Tippecanoe County Indiana

PERRY M. O'BRIEN
Born 6/11/1881   **Died**   1932 **[51]** (Momence Cemetery)
Married Bertha O'Brien
Lived in Gary, Indiana
Attended Pat's funeral with his wife

BERTHA O'Brien
Born 5/31/1881   **Died** 9/04/1970
Married Perry O'Brien
Died in Hammond, Lake Co, Indiana

> From email from Les Laskey, now deceased, dated May 23, 2008)
>
> *"Perry M. Obrien was married to Bertha Obrien. Their fathers were half-brothers. I never met Perry. We used to go and see Aunt Bertha many times in Gary Ind. My mother helped her in her later years. As my mother lived in Hammond Ind."*
>
> Mother refers to Marie O'Brien Laskey
>
> **Perry's** PARENTS were MARTIN O'BRIEN and AMY HURLEY O'BRIEN .Amy Hurley widow of Thomas Hurley.
> Bertha's PARENTS were William L and Julia Ann (Saylor) O'Brien.
> Bertha's Grandparents were *Martin* and Sarah (Ruggles) O'Brien
> Perry's Grandparents were Martin and Amy (Hurley) O'Brien

MERWIN "BUCK" J. O'BRIEN
Born 11/14/1885   **Died** 12/02/1969
Married   Merwin never married.
Lived in California (at the time of Margaret's death)
Never married. Did not attend Pat's funeral because he was "detained in California seeing to Pat's affairs"

CLARENCE "BUD" C. O'BRIEN
Born 7/29/1888   **Died**   12/30/1940 **[53]** (Momence Cemetery)
Married   Unknown
Attended Pat's funeral
Attended Margaret's funeral
In 1935 lived Los Angeles, CA, dishwasher.
At time of Margaret's death lived in Hammond, IN

ALVA P. "PAT" O'BRIEN
Born 12/13/1890 **Died** 12/17/1920 **[30]** (Momence Cemetery)
Married - Virginia Dale 1/1/1920

FOREST R. O'BRIEN
Born 11/28/1894 **Died** 2/10/1898 **[3.5]** (Momence Cemetery)

IVAN "MULLIGAN" M. O'BRIEN
Born 11/13/1896 **Died** 11/14/1962
Married 1st Wife   Alma Jensen December 1918
  Children
  Patricia P. 1919-1969 (named after Pat)
  Daniel O' Brien 1921-
  Merwin "Jack" O'Brien   9/14/1923 - 6/15/2015
  Frank O'Brien   1924-

  2nd Wife - Mabel

After Alma's death the children were raised by maternal grandparents Carl and Christiana Jensen, who had other children between ages 7 and `17. Died in Crown Point, IN. Lived with Margaret at the time of Pat's death) Attended Pat's funeral

"Maggie" and her children in 1918.
Back row, L to R: Perry, Clarence, Pat, Ivan, Merwin
First row, L to R: Lila (Mrs. Ben Worley), Maggie, Clara (Mrs. Matt Clegg)

**Daniel Martin Memorial December 7, 1901
Pat was eleven when his father died**

Daughters of Rebekah ~ Momence Chapter
Margaret O'Brien (top left)

Part II

Growing up Fearless

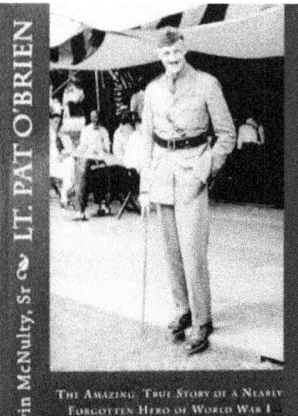

Chapter Reference

PART II ~ Growing up Fearless

Corresponding Chapters in "Lt. Pat O'Brien"

Chapter 8 Alva F. O'Brien	82
Chapter 9 Crawdadden'	92
Chapter 10 The Quarry	103
Chapter 11 The Beginnings of Flight	113
Chapter 12 Cody Wyoming	127
Chapter 13 The Lure of Chicago	136

PART II ~ Growing up Fearless Are great men born or are they shaped by the world around them? Are they anointed by the gods as the ancients believe or chosen by God himself as Royal nineteenth century Europe held? Perhaps it is the man himself who rises to greatness out of pure determination and faith. It is this archetype of the self-made man that so deeply inhabits in the American psyche.

Yet a fearless man never tested is mere bluster. A self-perceived leader, who has never met someone greater than himself, is delusional. And a man who believes admiration is due him unearned is admired by himself, alone. Pat's greatness was a result of his nature but it was also a product of his upbringing and the circumstances of his time.

Clearly, Pat O'Brien had something special. He also lived in a uniquely American town at a unique moment in history. From a very early age, family, friends, and residents of Momence recognized his aversion to risk and zest for living. But it was also the dynamic nature of frontier Momence, meeting the onslaught of the 20th Century America that gave Pat a platform to test his will.

Finding Pat O'Brien involved more than locating evidence of his many adventures or validating word-of-mouth tales of his greatness. It was always about understanding how this young, fatherless "Huck Finn," sent off to find his life at sixteen, mastered the art of aviation and grew up a patriot. In the end, it was his vision and desire to act that caused him to leave the U.S. Signal Corps and fight for the British against the Hun. He never considered staying captured when downed behind enemy lines. And he refused to believe that he could not reconcile with his wife who likely never loved him. Proving that war spares no one, Pat's untimely and controversial death at age thirty left open questions about the nature of great men and the delusions of tragic heroes we all admire.

from
**Lt. Pat O'Brien
Chapter 11
Page 117**

He liked to pop in on the Wennerholms and watch the mechanics work on engines. His conversation with the Wennerholm Brothers often turned toward the feasibility of placing an engine on a winged glider but he got little affirmation from the men in the shop. They knew little of these "new-fangled contraptions" and thought it "unnatural" for a human being to be "trying to fly around with the damn birds!"

The new Momence Agricultural Museum incorporated the façade of the Wennerholm Livery

Pat O'Brien and the Wennerholm Livery Stable ~ As a young boy, Pat O'Brien spent many days circulating throughout downtown Momence. From the Central House Hotel, where he bussed tables, to Astle's Hardware on Front Street to one of his favorite spots, the Wennerholm Livery Stable. About the time Wennerholms introduced the first automobile to Momence (a Jackson) Pat would often hang around and argue that the same engines used to power cars would allow man to fly. The old-timers laughed and enjoyed ribbing him over his wild imagination.

When Pat returned home following his miraculous escape from Germany after crashing his Sopwith Pup aeroplane, the town of Momence cleared and cleaned the Wennerholm Livery for his "Welcome Home" reception. Over 450 Momence residents heard is captivating story for the first time. There were many gasps and tears of joy that night.

Today, through the donations of a private citizen, Momence opened a museum on the same location, cleverly incorporating the original Wennerholm front façade in the new building design

Astle's Hardware in Pat's time

Astle's Hardware 2014

Most summer days he could be seen bolting out the front door on a mission to explore the wonders of the burgeoning little city of Momence. "Well that figures," Astle said in an audible voice. "Only you could chew up a walkway like a bull." The hardware man had a big grin on his face as he put his scuffed fists along each side. "Where the heck you goin' so early young Pat?"

from **"Lt. Pat O'Brien" Chapter 10 - Page 107**

The Quarry 1904

The Quarry

"Wait a minute! Where you boys fishin' today?" Astle asked. "The river?"

Pat froze. "Heck no - today we're going to the Quarry. Didn't yah hear? The whole thing filled up with water from the river!" Pat said with a big grin on his face. Then he waved and broke again with a joyful look only a thirteen year old could deploy. The railroad had shut down the limestone operation in early 1904. With pumps off, the deep hole quickly filled in with water.

from **"Lt. Pat O'Brien" Chapter 19, Page 108**

The Quarry 2014

The limestone quarry on the south side of Momence was mined for a number of years until water filled in. Pat won a bet that he could swim its length, faking a fainting spell on the opposite bank before delivering a "gotcha" to his concerned buddies. Pat often stated how important swimming as a youth was to his escape.

The Fontaines ~ No one was closer to Pat O'Brien than Albert Fontaine. The two boys were always together. Al was the quieter of the two for sure but their friendship extended into their adult years. Albert is the young boy in the first row on the far right.

Central School

No records were found of Pat's school attendance but we speculate he probably completed 8th grade and perhaps part of 9th.

He was a handful to Margaret but a true joy to her at the same time. His 8th grade teacher wrote in Pat's yearend report that he was a "loveable trial to his grade school teachers." Pat didn't have much time for school books but performed rather well and had sights well beyond the limitations of Central School.

from **"Lt. Pat O'Brien**

Jumping on Trains ~ *During the summer of 1906, young Pat O'Brien was fifteen years old. Having spent the previous summer visiting relatives by jumping on the train to Lowell, he migrated to the "big line," the C&EI, which ran north. An explosion of civilization the size of Chicago and its surroundings did not go unnoticed by the highly curious Pat O'Brien. Bored with most of Central School's routine, he spent a lot of time reading but he read newspapers, books from the library and anything he could find about the Wright Brothers' successes at Kitty Hawk in 1903.* from **"Lt. Pat O'Brien," Chapter 11, Page 118**

Columbia House ~ Across from the C&EI Railroad Depot stood Columbia House where it is believed Daniel proposed to Margaret. The O'Briens, Hathaways and Hansens all had lunch with Pat here before he boarded the train for Chicago, Toronto and England to join the war as British officer in the Royal Flying Corps.

"Lt. Pat O'Brien" Timeline

1830 - 1910

1830	Martin O'Brien enters the United States
1846	Daniel O'Brien is born
1853	Margaret Hathaway is born
1865	Daniel O'Brien is discharged from the Army
1872	Daniel O'Brien marries Margaret Hathaway
1887	C&EI Railroad donates Island Park to Momence
1890	Alva F "Pat" O'Brien is born
1901	Daniel O'Brien dies in his home (December 7)
1901	Pat O'Brien's 11th birthday (December 13)
1902	Charles Lindberg born in Detroit
1903	Margaret builds house at Hill and River Streets Wright Brothers succeed at Kitty Hawk
1906	Pat is sent to Cody, Wyoming to live with aunt Perry Hathaway dies
1909	Momence Civil War statue is erected

Part III

Flying Machines

Chapter Reference

PART III ~ Flying Machines

Corresponding Chapters in "Lt. Pat O'Brien"

Chapter 14	West Pullman	147
Chapter 15	Santa Fe	160
Chapter 16	The Unrelated Perturbation	172
Chapter 17	Signal Corps	189
Chapter 18	Pack up Your Troubles	202
Chapter 19	Canadian Crossing	215
Chapter 20	Mallards in Formation	227
Chapter 21	An Urgent Flurry	242

Flying Machines ~ After spending most of 1908 and 1909 living in Cody Wyoming, Pat had become increasingly restless. Though he appreciated the support of his aunts and uncles, he was unsettled. Since the Wright brothers success at Kitty Hawk in 1903, hundreds of would be inventors, engineers and daredevil test pilots, many his age, were racing to become the next successful aeroplane designers. Pat returned home on December 23, 1909.

After spending the holidays with family, he decided to move to San Joaquin Valley, California and help his brother farm. He met Ed Hesser, an amateur aeroplane buff and the two became friends, building a number of experimental aircraft, crashing more than once. Pat's time with Ed fueled his desire to learn all he could about aviation. In August of 1912, he read about a fantastic airshow scheduled for Chicago's Grant Park, featuring the country's top pilots. Pat left California the next day. Following the show, he revealed to Margaret that he would stay in Momence and attend the newly established flight school at West Pullman in Chicago. After a year of what was his first real flight training, he had acquired the reputation as a skilled and intuitive pilot

He returned to California. This time Richmond, where he got a job as a fireman on the Santa Fe Railroad. It was a good job and supported his passion to fly airplanes on the weekends as a test pilot for Joe Cato and others. It was here also that he met the most important person in his live, Agnes MacMillan. Agnes was a stylish, strong city woman who fell in love with Pat the moment she saw him. They spent two years together amid a growing number of friends. It was the highlight of his young adult life. But with the ever increased deaths of young test pilots across the country, aviation was shifting to the military. And with war in Europe and the U.S. surely joining the fight soon, Pat left for the Army Signal Corps at North Island near San Diego. They were designated to test the feasibility of the aeroplane as a weapon of war. Pat was among the first pilots to test the new Curtiss war machines. But he would grow impatient with the U.S. Army and eventually join the Canadians in their battle for Europe.

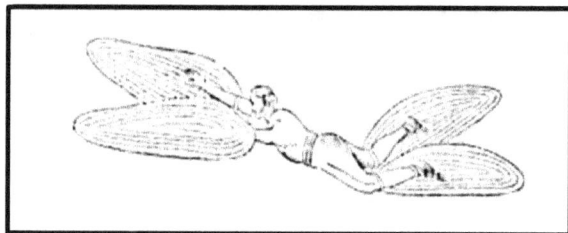

1747

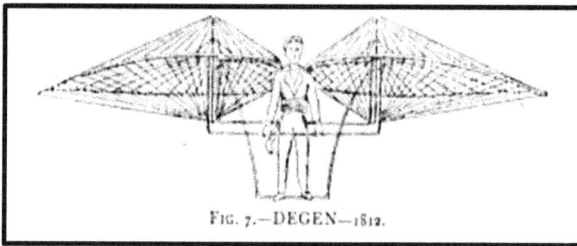

1812

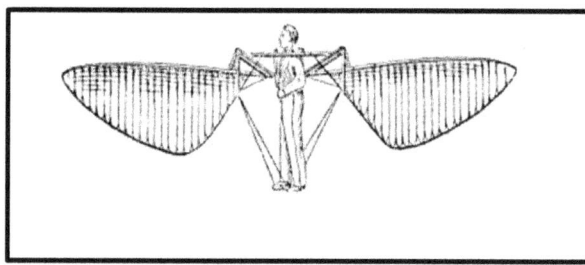

1879

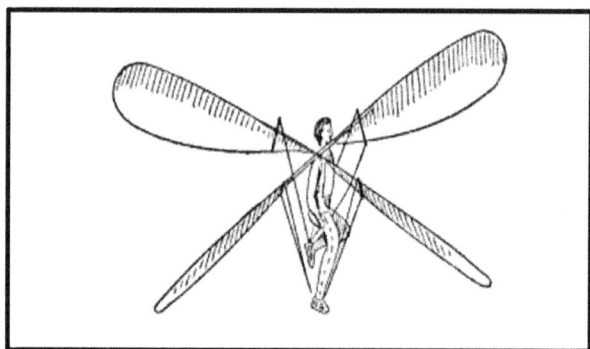

1886

from   **"Lt. Pat O'Brien"**
Chapter 11, Page 117

Pat and his friends talked about flying a lot. On a hot day, one could see the boys running along the trestle like a runway then leaping with arms extended out, bellies exposed to the shallow north branch simulating "man in flight." In the fall when school started one of Pat's teachers, knowing of his keen interest in the new idea of flying, gave Pat a small pamphlet highlighting Octave Chanute's 1894 publication called Progress in Flying Machines. The teacher had acquired it at the 1893 Chicago World's Fair.

The new mode of transportation went barely noticed amid the hundreds of special meetings held at the Chicago World's Fair. A French immigrant engineer, with roots in rail and bridge construction, held the world's first global conference at the Chicago World's Fair on the feasibility of controlled man flight. He discussed his planned testing of wings and gliders on the unblemished shores of Lake Michigan at Miller Beach. From the Fair's location on Lake Michigan's western rim, the white dunes of Indiana could be clearly seen if one looked southeast to southern shore which curved east into the neighboring state of Indiana.

"That's very near here, Al!" said Pat as the two boys read the paper together.
Octave Chanute was convinced it was only a matter of time before man would learn to fly. When he, his partner Augusta Herring and his three assistants climbed off the Michigan Central Railroad train at Miller Junction, Indiana on June 22, 1896, they attracted a good deal of attention. They walked the mile or so to the beach through downtown Miller from the train. They carried camping equipment, two gliders, and a kite.

From **"Lt. Pat O'Brien," Chapter 14, Page 149**
Like so many amateurs of the day, Pat's experience constructing and flying planes was self-taught and rather happenstance. The new flight school at West Pullman would be his opportunity to learn the principles of flying from some of the most experienced pilots of the day. The involvement of established manufacturers at the Cicero and West Pullman School assured that students were trained and tested on the latest equipment. Most early schools were opened by manufacturers and investors who attracted spirited youth to become the first test pilots. Flying was new and a natural aphrodisiac to the young who are always drawn to novelty with no concern for risk. Coincidentally, these were the same "indestructible" youth that so often march off to war. No war existed for this generation in 1912. Not yet.

Peter Christman, an 18 year old boy, of Green Bay, Wis., has built a monoplane which will be tried out in a few days. He will have it on exhibition at the Winnebago County Fair, Oshkosh, Wis.

An inventor in Racine, Wis., Martin Rasmussen, has a new machine ready for trial. It has an arrangement of planes and parachutes which it is said makes a sudden drop impossible.

Beckwith Havens, one of the latest to join the Curtiss squad, won $2,007 for the Curtiss Company flying at Chippewa Falls, Wis., the week of July 17.

The Curtiss-type biplane, built in Danville, Ill., by Charles Baysdorfer and Claude J. Coddington, has been shipped to Mineóla, L. I., for trial flights. The machine, it is said, could have been assembled for

1911
Chicago International
Aviation Meet

Lincoln Beachey

"Lt. Pat O'Brien"
Timeline
1906-1917

1906	Pat turns sixteen on December 13, no longer eligible for Daniel's military benefits
	Perry Hathaway dies in Momence
	In Spring Pat leaves with John Hansen to live in Wyoming
1909	Pat returns to Momence for Christmas
1910	Pat moves to California to live with Elmer
1911	Pat comes home to Momence in July
	Pat attends the International Aviation Meet in Chicago
1912	Pat attends Flying school at West Pullman in Chicago
1913	Pat heads back to California in March, this time to Richmond and a job with the Santa Fe Railroad.
1914	World War I begins in July
	Pat meets Agnes MacMillan in December
1915	Pat and Agnes attend Panama Pacific Exposition at Presidio. Pat witnesses the death of Lincoln Beachey
1916	January Pat tells Agnes he's joining the Signal Corps
	Pat says "good bye" to Alice and joins Canadian Corps
1917	After a two week leave in Momence, Pat says, "good bye" and heads for England
1917	Pat arrives in Liverpool on June 28

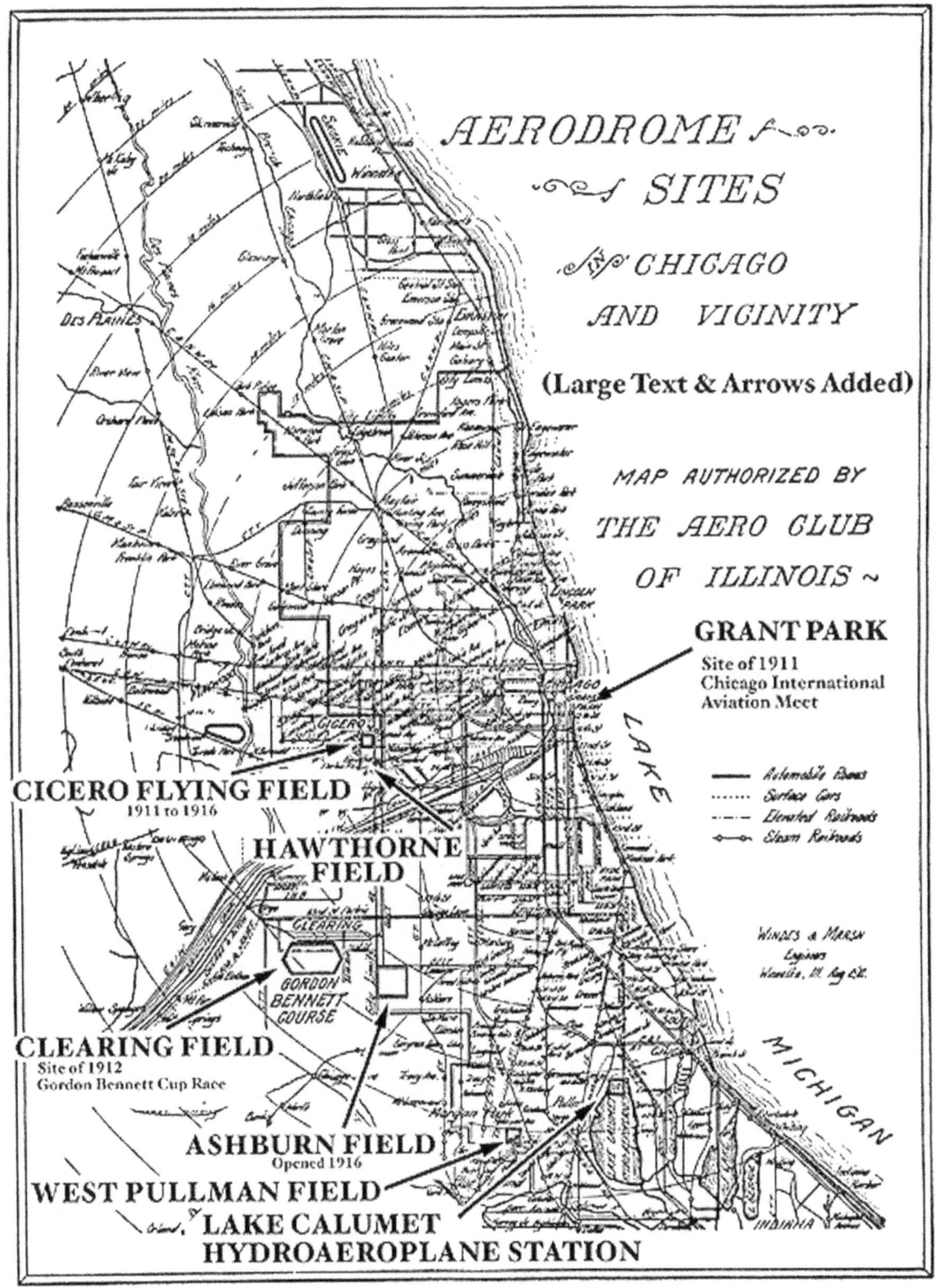

In Memoriam

Aviator's Neck Broken.
Machine Falls with Paul Peck, at Chicago,
Knoxville Daily Journal and Tribune
Knoxville, Tennessee: September 12, 1912

Chicago, Sept. 11 - Aviator Paul Peck of Washington, D.C., holder of the American duration flight record, was killed in a fall with a biplane tonight while flying in a gusty wind. He attempted too steep a spiral and when he struck the ground the heavy engine crushed through the wreckage, striking him in the neck.

A gusty wind blew at Cicero field all day and Director Andrew Drew posted the customary warning to aviators against going up. Peck, believing his small biplane would be fast enough to carry him through the choppy wind, went into the air in spite of the caution.

At about eight hundred feet altitude, he started to come down in a spiral glide. Because of the unusually small span of his machine, Peck got into too steep a spiral, his aeroplane slid in toward the center of the vortex, and he could not bring it back. [We know today that you must first roll with the ailerons and rudder to level the wings before you pull back on the stick to pull the nose up with the elevator.]

His real difficulty did not become apparent till he was within 200 feet of the ground. He would have escaped with minor injuries, Director Drew and his technical committee declared, had it not been for the fact that the heavy engine, crashing through the framework, with its gasoline tank and iron fittings, struck Peck in the neck and across the legs. He died an hour later in St. Anthony de Padua hospital.

Peck was American licensed aviator No. 57 and [he] had developed a monoplane and the biplane in which he was killed. The biplane was of only 26 feet span, headless [no elevator in front] and equipped with a Gyro motor. He was about twenty-four years old and was making a trial flight preparatory for the international aviation meet here tomorrow. Twenty-four American and foreign aviators will meet tomorrow on the Cicero **flying**

From
"Lt. Pat O'Brien," Chapter 14, Page 149

The 1913 exhibition season was anticipated with some dread. It was widely assumed that the peak of such activities had passed, and great concern was expressed over the enormous number deaths of aviators which were occurring with sad frequency. These were young kids losing their lives. Even so, some 1,200 real aerial exhibitions were given that year.

Another trend exacerbated the downward spiral of exhibition flying. A significant number of intentional frauds, using phony aviators, took gate receipts to shows and "flew" in an earth-bound sense, on the next train out of town. Promoters of fake exhibitions stalked

On July 12, 1973, a disastrous fire at the National Personnel Records Center in St. Louis destroyed approximately 16-18 million Official Military Personnel Files. The records affected included 80% of Army Personnel discharged November 1 1912 to January 1 1960. All records of Pat O'Brien's service in the Army Signal Corps were lost.

The loss of U.S. Army records frustrated Momence citizen's efforts to place a United States Army marker on Pat's grave. In our research we discovered a San Diego voting record that strong indicted that Pat served in the Army Signal Corps and was entitled to an official bronze military marker.

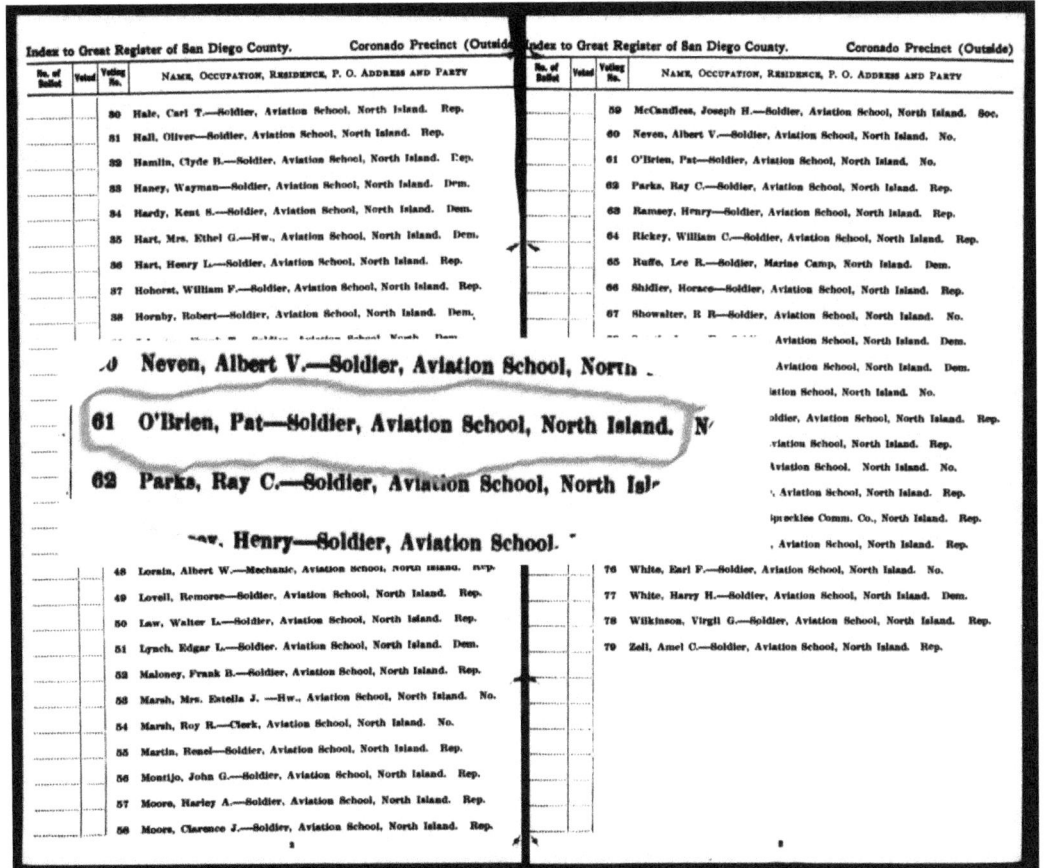

Additional evidence of Pat's service in the Army Signal Corps and his presence at North Island during the very early days of U.S. Military Aviation appeared in the Nov-Dec *San Diego Flying Days* newsletter in 1917. By that time, Pat had become famous across the country for his escape from German hands. A member of the local aviation club submitted his memories of Pat when he served in the Signal Corps and was known as a crafty shooter of craps. It was known that Perry Hathaway, Pat's grandfather, taught him to shoot craps during the time following Daniel's death.

San Diego Flying Days, November-December 1917, Issue
Editor's note: Pat served in the 66th Squadron of the Royal Flying

```
   Pat O'Brien made headlines around the country. In July 1916 he
had been a Private First Class at North Island. After receiving
an honorable discharge he had enlisted in the Royal Canadian
Flying Corps. After becoming an aviator with the 3rd Squadron,
Lt O'Brien was shot down and interned in a German camp. He had
escaped and made his way back to the Allies. Newspapers made him
a hero. At San Diego most of his acquaintances remembered him as
a champion crap-shooter. His luck was still holding out.
```

The Wright Brother's Plane is delivered to Fort Mill, Virginia for testing as the first Military Aircraft

CAMP BORDEN TORONTO, CANADA

In 1917, the Royal Flying Corps decided to establish a training organization in Canada. The plan called for three stations: RFC Station Camp Borden, RFC Station Desoronto and RFC Station North Toronto. The camp was hurriedly constructed, opened on May 2, 1917 and Pat arrived in June. It was the first flying station to begin full-scale operations and it was the largest of the Royal Flying Corps fields in Canada. From 1917-1919 Camp Borden was the chief training center in Canada for the Royal Flying Corps and later, the Royal Air Force.

From "Lt. Pat O'Brien," Chapter 20, Page 237 *He spent his last hour at home on the porch telling Margaret where he would go in England. He described the many steps he would take before earning his wings, his likely flights over France, and his excitement about getting into the fight. Like all mothers, it all seemed too overwhelming and the prospect of Pat flying into combat distressed her to no end. Still she offered encouraging words and forced a smile in response to Pat's excitement.*

Pat and his good friend Paul Raney sail to England to fight the Hun

Meeting Hall where Pat and Paul first met in Toronto.

From "Lt. Pat O'Brien, Chapter 20, Page 240

The eighteen pilots that made up two flights "A" and "B" were bound for St. John, New Brunswick. Nine of the flyers were British subjects and the other nine were Americans. This first batch of Borden trained pilots all had previous experience flying which accounted for the large contingent of Americans. Like Pat, they had joined the Royal Flying Corps impatient to join the action. All but one Canadian pilot, H.K. Boysen, was saying good-bye to relatives on the platform. Boysen was from western Canada and had said his goodbyes at home in much the same way as had Pat.

The two exchanged a good deal about their background, families, and adventures to date. Paul Raney was from Toronto and had just graduated from the University of Toronto the past May. He decided to join the Imperial Royal Flying Corp right out of school.

Rare and never before seen photo of Pat O'Brien and his best chum Paul Raney from Toronto Canada. The two were best friends, having trained together at Camp Borden in Canada. While recovering from his wounds in a German field hospital behind enemy lines, Pat witnessed the death of his best friend in a "dog fight" overhead. This is the last known photo of Pat and Paul, both in full gear and standing front of a plane. - Appeared in the Lincoln, Nebraska, Star, April 28, 1918.

Part IV

Sudden Folly

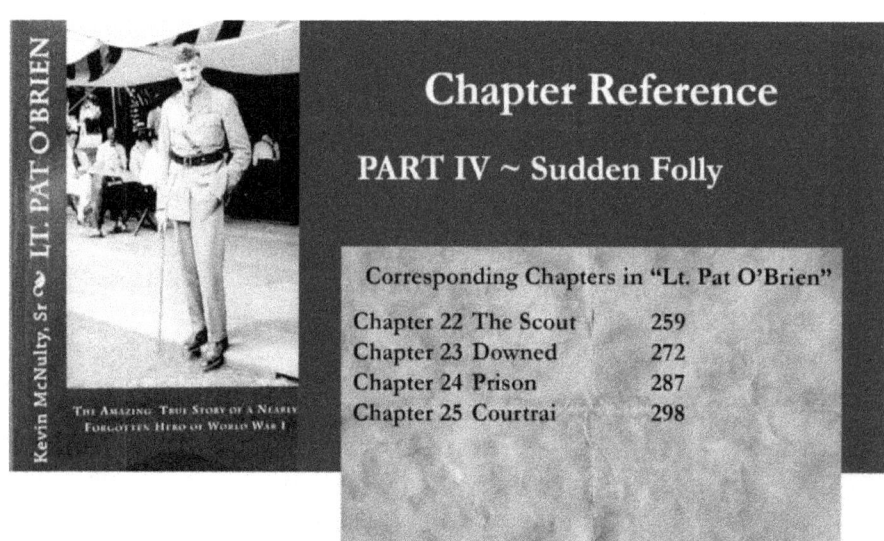

Sudden Folly ~ Sailing from St. John to Liverpool, England in 1917 was not without peril. The ship SS Megantic was forced to make numerous zig-zag maneuvers in order to avoid attacks from German U-Boats. Pat O'Brien, and the other seventeen pilots on board, were rightly unnerved by the experience. They were untested soldiers. The trip abroad was nothing compared to what all of them would experience shortly.

Each pilot was an expert flyer but training in England involved something new. They would learn to become warriors and use their airplanes as they never had before. The English had been tested and knew how to use the airplane as a weapon.

No sooner had Pat and his group earned their wings, they were off to France and the Pilots Pool Mess where "raw meat" was tossed in the direction of Germany as quickly as the dead returned. Each time the call-bell rang, Pat rushed to report but his name was not on the list. Finally, on August 12, his name appeared. Little did he know that his career as a fighter pilot would last a mere five days. On August 17, he was shot through the jaw at 8,000 feet and crashed. He survived both the crash and harsh surgery performed on him by a hateful German surgeon.

In his first week of recovery, he witnessed the death of his best friend Paul Raney. He was imprisoned for three weeks before the Germans loaded Pat and other officers on a train for the interior. In the early morning hours of September 9, less than a month from his crash, Pat leapt from the prison train and escaped. It would take him seventy-two days to reach the Holland border and appear in the London, to the amazement of his British officers.

"Lt. Pat O'Brien" Timeline
July 24 - September 7, 1917

July 24	Pat earns his wings in England, now a 2nd Lieutenant
July 28	Pat, Paul and six others in his flight land their Sopwith Pup airplanes in France.
August 12-17	Pat's flights over Europe

          August 12   1st Flight
          August 13   2nd Flight
                             3rd Flight
          August 16   4th Flight
                             5th Flight
                             6th Flight
          August 17   7th Flight
                             8th Flight   Did not return

August 21	Pat sends postcard home, "I am a POW" Paul Raney dies in a dog fight
August 25	Pat enters prison at Courtrai
August 27	Prison photo taken that appears in Pat's book
September 2	Pat and other prisoners paraded through town
September 4	Pat awakes in the middle of the night at Courtrai Prison infected by lice. He spends the night at the fumigation building
September 7	After hording food for three days, Pat plots escape with fellow prisoners but they get "cold feet".

MERCHANT SHIPPING ACT, 1906, AND ALIENS ACT, 1905.

IN-COMING PASSENGERS.

Returns of Passengers brought to the United Kingdom in ships arriving from Places out of Europe, and not within the Mediterranean Sea

NAMES AND DESCRIPTIONS OF **BRITISH** PASSENGERS

Name in book Pat's Book	Name on Manifest
Nine Americans	
C. C. Robinson	Charles C. Robinson
H. A. Miller	Harvey A. Miller
F. S. McClurg	Frank S. McClurg
A. A. Allen	Albert A. Allen
E. B. Garnett	Evanda A. Allen
H. K. Boysen	Harold K. Boysen
H. A. Smeeton	Harold K. Smeeton
A. Taylor	Alford Taylor
Pat O'Brien	Pat O'Brien
Nine British	
Paul H. Raney	Paul H. Raney
J. R. Park	John R. Park
C. Nelmes	Cyril Nelmes
C. R. Moore	Charles R. Moore
T. L. Atkinson	Thomas L. Atkinson
F. C. Conry	Francis C. Conry
A. Muir	Archie Muir
E. A. L. F. Smith	Emerson Smith
A. C. Jones	Arthur C. Jones

Official record of Pat O'Brien and Paul Raney onboard ship to Liverpool England along with sixteen other pilots trained at Borden

SS Megantic
Ship's Manifest
Arrival - June 27, 1917

66th Squadron, Royal Flying Corps

Courtesy of
John Grech, Researcher and Historian for the 66th Squadron
Royal Flying Corps in England,

Pat O'Brien's activity in England upon arrival

"After arriving in England they all underwent further flying training. On gaining his wings Pat was awarded Royal Aero Club certificate 5397 on 16 June 1917, he gave his home address as 43 Powell Street, San Francisco, California. Pat was sent to 23 (Training) Wing in England arriving on 28 June 1917. 23 Wing's main aerodrome was at South Carlton with a half flight at Thetford. By the 20 July 1917 he had been posted to Reading and 1 School of Instruction. His record indicates that he was then posted to 81 Squadron on 25 July, although 81 Squadron was not officially due to form at Scampton as a training unit until 1 August 1917 under the control of 23 Wing, but Pat O'Brien was posted to 66 Squadron via the Pilots Pool in France on 28 July 1917."

66th Squadron Activity

"Pat joined 66 on 28 July along with Edgar H. Garland from New Zealand and Charles. H. F. Nobbs from Norfolk Island Australia. Garland was shot down on 22 August when his Scout's engine failed and would later attempt to escape Nobbs was shot down on 20 September and like Pat became prisoners of war. Pats first flight with 66 Squadron was on the evening of the 12 August when he flew B1710 with New Zealander Ralph Steadman and his friend from training days in Canada Paul Raney, in his book Pat notes that he was "taken over the lines to get a look at things". The next day, 13 August, he had a morning practice flight, along with William Keast and Paul Raney arriving back at the aerodrome at 08.40 a.m. His first combat patrol was made later the same day when along with patrol leader, Evelyn H Lascelles, Ralph Stedman, Frank S Wilkins and William Keast they undertook the squadrons 3rd patrol of the day."

"On the 16 August patrol leader Angus Bell-Irving led Paul Raney, Pat in B1732, Ralph Stedman, William Keast and Evelyn Lascelles on the first patrol of the day. Lascelles dropped out of the formation around 9 a.m. with gun problems landing at 1 squadron's aerodrome at Bailleul (Asylum Ground), 30 minutes later Pat dropped out of the patrol landing at 100 squadron's home at Treizennes with engine trouble. He departed 100 squadron at 11.30 a.m. arriving 66 squadron at 1.50 p.m. a flight of some 2hrs 20 minutes although the distance if some 5-6 Kms."

"Pat in his book states that "After doing our regular patrol, it was our privilege to go off on our own hook, if we wished, before going back to the squadron" later on page 21 he retells the events of the 17 August, his claim of a two seater and notes that he saw "two German balloons and decided to go off on his own hook and see what a German balloon looked like at close quarters". Does this account for the time he took to return to his home aerodrome the previous day, if he did go of on his own hook the flight should still have been recorded in the squadron record book, even then, would an experienced Squadron Commander like Boyd let a new recruit go off on his own over the Lines? Later on page 23 he says "When our two hours duty was up, therefore, I dropped out of the formation as we crossed the lines and turned back again". "

"There is no possibility of the Sopwith Scout having a combat endurance of some four hours or more. I suspect that the flight probably took place on the 16 whilst making his way back from 100 Sqn. On 17 August, Pat on his first patrol of the day, claimed an unidentified reconnaissance C type but later in the evening, after shooting down an unidentified D-type Scout he was in turn shot down, sustaining a gunshot wound to his neck crashing behind the German lines and became a prisoner of war. Pat was quite close to 2/Lt Paul Raney who signed for Pat's personal belongings and sent them back to Cox & Co the RFC Bankers in England. The McKean County Miner (20 June 1918) newspaper carried a photograph of the document and Pat mentions it in his book. He also claims to have witnessed the dogfight of the 21 August when his friend and traveling companion Paul Raney was shot down and killed, possibly by Ltn Weiss of Jasta 28. Also shot down that day and killed was 2/Lt. William R Keast (In his book O'Brien mistakenly calls him "Keith" from Australia, he was a native of Carlton, Victoria, Australia, although his parents lived in Brighton, Melbourne, Australia.) Keast is commemorated on the Arras Memorial."

The Sopwith Pup - Plane flown by Pat O'Brien over Germany

The PUP ~*The Sopwith Pup was a British single-seater biplane fighter aircraft built by the Sopwith Aviation Company. It entered service with the Royal Flying Corps and the Royal Naval Air Service in the autumn of 1916. With pleasant flying characteristics and good maneuverability, the aircraft proved very successful.*

Pat shown in a "two-seater" after the war, likely while on tour. He crashed such a plane in Dallas after the war while performing a demonstration for the troops. Note his autograph on the photo. This is the only known photo of Pat in a plane.

From "Lt. Pat O'Brien," Chapter 23, Page 294

Then it hit. No sound, no warning, just an intense heat in his mouth and in his throat. The same gun that obliterated Pat's dash board had found Pat. The bullet entered from above, passing through his upper lip, out the roof of his mouth and lodging in his throat. Adrenaline rushed throughout Pat's body. It stung more than hurt in the first few seconds. The bullet sliced close to the carotid artery but did not sever it. It lodged against the trachea avoiding any penetration of the spinal area. No doubt the bullet's path from above, passing through the upper lip, teeth and gum curtailed its ability to pass deeper and deliver a deadly blow.

He suddenly went dark. Then alert for a few seconds. The plane's roar stirred his consciousness. "Pull up…" he thought. "Wait, no…what is that?" Then out again, falling rapidly and spinning. Then wind. Wind in his face. His mind went back to the plane "Pull up!" "Pull!" More speed, descending with force. Sensing his hands, then… "Pull!" Then black. Then awake. "Oh, it hurts there…there…my face…no, it's my mouth." And Back to plane, "How fast am I…..It's quiet." Then Out.

Coast Aviator Missing.

Victoria, B.C., Sept. 25.—Flight Lieut. Pat O'Brien, aged 22, who came here from the Mexican border to offer his services as a pilot in the Royal Flying corps, is missing. About two months ago he left Canada for overseas.

First Reports~ After the crash and during the month that Pat was in captivity, few newspapers reported his circumstances. But after his miraculous appearance seventy-two days later, the press could not get enough of war hero, Pat O'Brien

RICHMOND MAN SICK IN GERMAN PRISON CAMP

RICHMOND, Nov. 16.—Wounded, sick and suffering in a German prison camp, Pat O'Brien, former Santa Fe employee of this city, has written to friends here of his plight. Information as to O'Brien's situation was received yesterday on a postcard by John K. Keeton, 108 Chanslor avenue, a Santa Fe fireman. The words on the card written by O'Brien, said: "I am sick and wounded. Across the face of the card were printed the words: "Do not answer until further notified."

Pat O'Brien is a lieutenant in the Royal Flying Corps. After many sensational exploits for which he received decorations for bravery and coolness under fire he was captured on an expedition over the enemy lines. It was at first reported that he was killed, but the word received by Keeton yesterday confirms the report that he was captured.

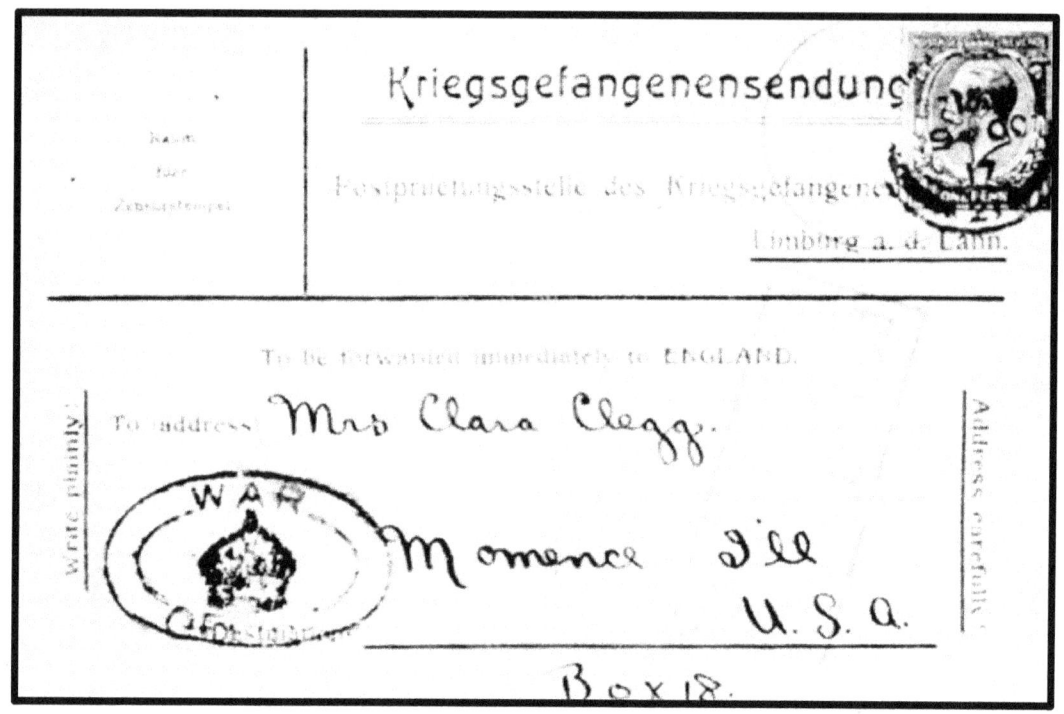

One of two postcards allowed by the Germans to be sent home by **Pat** when he was in prison. The other went to **Agnes**.

MY FALL INTO GERMANY FROM AN AEROPLANE.

"As he sailed along barely ten yards away I had 'the drop' on him, and he knew it."

Drawn by] [Geoffrey Watson.

OFFICIAL FLIGHT RECORD OF PAT O'BRIEN

2/LT PAT O'BRIEN 66 Squadron Flight Schedule

The flight record of 2/Lt. Pat O'Brien is provided through the courtesy of John Grech, Hinckley, Leicestershire, England. This record was obtained from the British Public Records Office (now The National Archives) on July 27, 2007

1st Flight 12/08/17   Practice flight
Sopwith Scout s/n*
* B1710 2/Lt P A O'Brien 7.50 – 8.10 pm A6190 2/Lt R.A. Stedman (Ralph) B1846 2/Lt P Raney

2nd Flight 13/08/17   Practice flight
B1775 2/Lt W.R. Keast 7.45 9.25 am
B1846 2/Lt P Raney B1710 2/Lt P. O'Brien

3rd flight 13/08/17   Patrol Number 3
B2176 Lt E.H. Lascelles B1846 2/LT P.A. O'Brien
A6190 2/Lt R.A. Stedman A6212 Lt F.S. Wilkins B1775 2/Lt W.R. Keast

4th flight 16/08/17   Patrol No1 7.30-9.05 am
B1733 Capt A Bell-Irving B1846 2/Lt P Raney
B1732 2/Lt P A Obrien 7.30-9.30 engine trouble landed at 100 sqn
A6190 2/Lt R.A.Stedman B1775 2/Lt W.R. Keast
    B2176 Lt E.H. Lascelles, landed 1 Sqn gun trouble

5th flight 16/08/17
B1732 2/Lt P.A. O'Brien returned from
100 Sqn 1130-1.50 pm

6th flight 16/08/17 Patrol No5 5.50-7.15 pm.
B1733 Capt A Bell-Irving returned engine trouble 1732 2/Lt P.A. O'Brien
B1846 2/Lt P Raney B2176 Lt E.H. Lascelles B1838 Lt B F.S. Wilkins

7th flight 17/08/17 Offensive Patrol No1 6.30-9.15 am A6242 2/Lt C.C. Morley
B2162 2/Lt F Huxley B1760 Lt T.V. Hunter B1838 Lt S. Harper B1732 2/Lt P.A. O'Brien
B1762 2/Lt W.A. Pritt returned engine trouble.

8th Flight 17/08/17 Patrol No2 5.45-8.35 pm B1733 Capt A. Bell-Irving
B1846 2/Lt P Raney B1775 2/Lt W.R. Keast
B1794 2/Lt E. Bacon returned engine trouble B2176 Lt E.H Lascelles
B1732 2/Lt P.A. O'Brien. **Not returned**

PAT'S LAST FLIGHT – ACTUAL RECORD

Date... 14th August, 1917.

No. 66 Squadron, Royal Flying Corps.

REPORT ON OFFENSIVE PATROL No. 2.

Area or line.	ROY .L . I - OF REAL.
No. & type of machines.	Six Sopwith Scouts.
Time of start	5-45 p.m.
A.A. Activity.	Normal.
E.A. Activity.	Above normal.
E.A. brought down and by whom.	One driven down completely out of control and one driven down damaged by Capt. Bell-Irving; two driven down by Lt. Lascelles, one probably out of control.
No. of combat reports attached.	Two.

Information concerning machines.

1. Returned 8-15 p.m. – engine trouble.
2. Returned 8-35 p.m.
3. -do-
4. -do-
5. -do-
6. Not yet returned.

7. B/1714 Lt. Bacon
8. B/1733 Capt. Bell-Irving
9. B/1846 Lt. Harvey
10. B/1775 Lt. Heast
11. B/2106 Lt. Lascelles
12. B/1732 Lt. O'Brien

REMARKS:

Patrol observed Bristol Fighters below them being attacked and went down to join the fight.

Major,
Commanding No.66 Squadron,
Royal Flying Corps.

Interview with 2nd Lieut. Pat Alva O'Brien,
66th Squadron, Royal Flying Corps.

5.A.

Momence,
Illinois,
U.S.A.

Captured 17th August, 1917, at Langemark.

I am an American and shall be 26 years of age in December 1917. I was in the employ of the Santa Fe Railway from 1909 until July 1916 when I joined the American Flying Corps. I obtained my discharge in January 1917, and 8 days afterwards I went to Victoria B.C., and joined the Royal Flying Corps with a view to being sent to the front. After training in Canada where I obtained my Commission I came over to England in June 1917 and trained at Scampton near Lincoln, Oxford, Reading and again at Lincoln. I went out to France early in July, going from Boulogne to St. Omer and thence to the 66th Squadron at Aire. I flew a single seater fighting machine (a Sopwith Pup Scout) and I had to go on patrol duties and engage enemy machines. I had made flights previous to 17th August, 1917, and on that day six of us went on patrol over the German lines. I had been up nearly 2½ hours and had only 10 minutes more duty when we were attacked by enemy machines which outnumbered us by two to one. I accounted for one machine before I myself was brought down. My propeller was hit and my petrol tank punctured, and I was hit in the lip by an explosive bullet. I could tell this by the sound of the machine guns. My motor stopped and I had to come down, and alighted, I believe in an infantry camp near Langemark, five miles behind the German lines. This was about 8p.m. and two other machines besides mine were brought down. I was knocked unconscious and when I came to I found myself in the Artillery Officers Headquarters.

The above extract has been taken from the original M.I.1.a Branch Memo No. 27880 dated 30-11-17.

War Office Confirms Pat

Whenever a soldier escapes it is standard proceedure for the War Department to take an official interview from the returning soldier. It is designed to confirm the nature of his story but more importantly its purpose is to make sure the escaped soldier is not a spy and that his story is true.

Pat's written statement is to the left. Below is the confirmation by three officers who interviewed him that he told the truth.

Pat describes the battle below left.

WAR OFFICE,
LONDON, S.W.1.

August 1919.

A.G.3.(P.W.)

The Secretary of the War Office presents his compliments

2nd Lieutenant P. A. O'Brien.

Royal Air Force.

and begs to state that he is commanded by the Army Council to inform him that his statement regarding the circumstances of his capture by the enemy having been investigated, the Council considers that no blame attaches to him in the matter.

The investigation was carried out by a Standing Committee of Enquiry composed as follows:—

Major-General L. A. E. Price-Davies, V.C., C.M.G., D.S.

Brigadier-General C. R. J. Griffith, C.B., C.M.G., D.S.O.

Brevet-Lieut. Col. E. L. Challenor, C.B., C.M.G., D.S.O.

"Eight of us started together and we had not been out very long when nine Hun machines came after us. We figured that with nine Huns to eight British or Americans the odds were easy, so we went.

"I know now that it was a trap. At the time, however, the fun was too great to think of giving up, so we went after them in a hurry. They kept retreating, firing an occasional shot to lead us on, until suddenly eleven machines rose, apparently from nowhere, and these eighteen Huns attacked the seven of us—for one of our boys had been dropped.

"For the first time I fought with bitterness in my heart. Up to this time I hadn't felt much hatred for the Hun. There was work to be done, and I did it, as cold-bloodedly as if I had been told that a pack of rats in the cellar must be chased and killed. You don't hate rats when you kill them, and that is how I felt toward the Hun up to that moment. With those odds against us, however, I began to hate them and I haven't stopped hating them yet.

"We had been fighting but a few minutes when they got me, the bullet going through the roof of my mouth and lodging in my throat. As I was hit, I must have shut off my motor, because if I hadn't, I should have been instantly killed, my fall being from 8,000 feet. As it was, I was only terribly bruised and broken up, and, of course, knocked unconscious."

IN PAT'S OWN WORDS

Courtrai ~ One of the most amazing photos in Pat O'Brien's best-selling book "Outwitting the Hun," was this group shot of the prisoners at Courtrai. It was taken by a guard. Somehow, Pat still had some money on his person and paid the guard for the photo. He then carried it with him all the way to freedom, including when he swam numerous streams, dikes and rivers. Pat is pictured in the center of the photo just over the German guard's right shoulder. One can still see "Smiling Pat" flashing what is for him a somewhat diminished grin. Below is Pat's ID which he also wore to freedom, shows he is an American flying for the British. From **"Outwitting the Hun," by Pat O'Brien.**

Part V

Determined Break

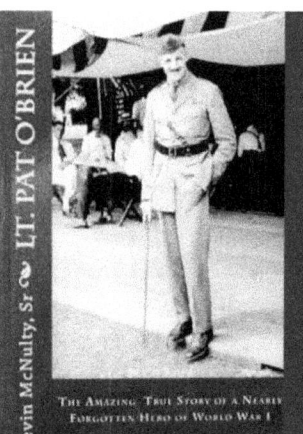

Chapter Reference

PART V ~ Determined Break

Corresponding Chapters in "Lt. Pat O'Brien"

Chapter	Title	Page
Chapter 26	Calculated Risk	308
Chapter 27	Mud, Blood and Stars	319
Chapter 28	Belgium	328
Chapter 29	Imposter	338
Chapter 30	Last Leg	351
Chapter 31	Holland	359
Chapter 32	London	369

```
FOR INFORMATION ONLY. NOT TO BE COMMUNICATED OUTSIDE THE WAR OFFICE.
                        No.X. 64699.
                        0103/1/841.

The following British Officer, Prisoner of War, is reported as having
escaped from Germany and arrived in the United Kingdom 21st November, 1917
                        ----------

2nd Lt. P.A. O'Brien.     Royal Flying Corps.
```

Determined Break ~ The prison at Courtrai was a difficult ordeal for Pat but nothing like he would experience once he escapes and walks through enemy territory for seventy-two days. Pat began plotting a way to escaped almost as soon as he was captured but failed to convince others in prison to join him. In the end, that was certainly best. Few could have sustained the long trip to the Holland boarder. Pat stated in his book "Outwitting the Hun" that he would have failed in his escaped had not spent his youth swimming in the Kankakee River and the Momence Quarry as a kid.

His leap to freedom came just days after he crashed from 8,000 feet. Indeed, he reinjured himself in the jump. Though his actual route is not known, the best estimate is that he walked 250 to 300 miles in seventy-two days. His encounters with friendly peasants and German guards are all documented in his book. Pat was highly reflective during his trip and he revealed many of his thoughts during the ordeal in speeches following the war.

It was in Holland that he me Janus Venansius who welcomed him into his home and gave him his first warm meal since the escape. Years later, one of the Venansius boys wrote a letter to Pat which arrived in Momence well after Pat's death.

Pats story captivated those that met him in the first few days of freedom. Despite his disheveled appearance he was able to convince the friendly Dutch and British officers that met him in London that he was a British officer. His story would captivate every person that heard him speak in 1918.

Stunning Illustrations ~ Naturally, there is no pictorial record of either Pat's escape or his 250 mile trek through Europe. Illustrators from "The Wide World Magazine" brought Pat's story to life with the following illustrations. Drawings on pages 69, 79 and 83 are also from the same magazine story published in 1918. "The Wide World Magazine" was a British monthly illustrated publication which ran from April 1898 to December 1965. An original copy of this issue went on eBay for $375 but the authors were unable to acquire it. These photos were taken from a black and white reprint published by Princeton University.

"I PULLED MYSELF UP, SHOVED MY FEET AND LEGS OUT OF THE WINDOW, AND LET GO!"
(SEE PAGE 10.)

TRAMPED 72 DAYS ESCAPING GERMANS

Lieut. O'Brien of Illinois Dodged Death Many Times in Flight from His Captors.

LEAPED FROM TRAIN IN DARK

Former Santa Fe Engineer Tunneled Under Live Wires with Bare Hands to Reach Holland.

Copyright © The New York Times
Originally published November 30, 1917

LONDON, Nov. 29.—Lieutenant Patrick O'Brien of Momence, Ill., south of Chicago, the first American member of the British Flying Corps to escape from Germany, has arrived in London. O'Brien eluded his captors by jumping from the window of a speeding train. He then became a fugitive for seventy-two days, and as his goal was within sight narrowly escaped electrocution from the charged wires along the Holland frontier.

After cabling to his aged mother, Mrs. Margaret O'Brien at Momence, to expect to see him soon, Lieutenant O'Brien called upon American Ambassador Page to seek advice regarding his desire to be transferred to the American Flying Corps. Last night O'Brien was dined by a group of admiring fliers, who, like scores of friends along the front, had believed he had been killed when he was reported missing on Aug. 17 last.

O'Brien, who is a sturdy man of 27, was flying in the American Aviation Squadron at San Diego, Cal., when he went to Victoria, B. C., and obtained a commission in the Canadian Army. Going to France the next year he distinguished himself by his great daring over the German lines. On the morning of Aug. 17 German gunners forced him to descend, but he landed behind his own lines.

Late that afternoon he went up again over the German lines, fighting the enemy. There were twenty German machines to six Brtish in the encounter, O'Brien's machine alone engaging four German craft and accounting for one before he was shot through the upper lip. He fell with his damaged airplane from a height of 8,000 feet. O'Brien says he cannot explain why he was not killed. When he regained consciousness he was in a German hospital.

Leaps From Train

"We rode all day and all night. Twice I put up the window to jump and lost my nerve. It looked too much like sudden death. As I put it up again, about four in the morning, the guard gave me an ugly look. I knew it was then or never and dove out.

"For nearly a month afterward I thought my left eye was gone. The scars are there yet. By the time the train stopped, a half-mile on, or more, I was up and stumbled to a hiding place. Those Germans looked everywhere—on the side of the tracks toward the border. I was in the opposite direction.

"It was a month before I got rid of my English uniform. I stole a pair of overalls one night. I got a cap the next and a shirt later. A Belgian gave me a scarf. That was all the help I got."

As an appetizer Lieutenant O'Brien ate turnip. The entree was sugar beet, and the meal closed with a cabbage stump that even the Germans scorned.

"And I never did like vegetables," he said. "I hope I never have to eat another."

One night a German soldier saw him swimming a river, and raised the alarm.

"I felt sure they would be on top of me in a few minutes," he said, "so I ran upstream and swam back to the other side. I knew the ways of the Hun pretty well by then. They looked everywhere on the other side, but not a German came near me.

Swam the Meuse

"One of the hardest things I did was to swim the Meuse river. I had all my clothes on, to my boots, and the river was half a mile across. It nearly got me twenty-five feet from shore. I was choking, and I admit praying. My boyhood on the Kankakee saved my life.

"When I got up the bank I fainted. It was the only time I ever fainted."

Lieutenant O'Brien could not speak German. As a boy, a Momence baker of Teuton origin taught him a phrase of German, but he did not know what it meant. It was some "ten lifetimes" after swimming the Meuse he found the nine-foot death fence of the Holland frontier. Death all but got him then, as his improvised ladder dropped him on the charged wires.

"A few minutes later," he said, "I could have tripped the guard with my ladder. After he had gone I dug—dug as I never dug before in my life. My back was half an inch from death when I crawled under and into Holland."

LOWELL AVIATOR ESCAPES FROM GERMAN PRISON

VOL. LXXXVIII—TWO CENTS—SUNDAY FIVE CENTS

Richmond Lad Escapes From German Prison; Makes Way Back Home

Richmond Birdman Visits King: Made Three Escapes

Famous Momence Aviator Who Escaped From Enemy

Lieut. Pat O'Brien of the Royal Flying Corps

AVIATOR DODGES HUNS 72 DAYS

Lieut. Pat. O'Brien of Illinois Tells of Wild Adventures in Germany.

JUMPS FROM MOVING TRAIN

TOWN OF MOMENCE HAS REAL WAR HERO

Lieut. Pat O'Brien Subject of Stirring Message Cabled From London

MOMENCE BOY RECEIVED BY ENGLAND'S KING

(By Associated Press)
London, Dec. 7—Flight Lieutenant Patrick O'Brien of Momence, a member of the British flying corps, arrived in London last week after having escaped from a German prison camp, was received by King George today at Buckingham pal[ace]

Headlines Explode in the Press

"Lt. Pat O'Brien" Timeline

1917 - September 8 - December 7

September 8	Pat jumps from prison train in Germany
September 12	Pat gets his first long sleep in the brush. He sleeps till dawn and awakes astounded that he is in the backyard of a German farmer. He is undetected.
September 18	Pat crosses into Luxemburg
September 26	Pat crosses into Belgium
September 28	(Approximate date) Pat approaches a small house in the country and asks for food for the first time.
October	Pat spends a few nights hiding in an abandoned house in Brussels
November 19	Pat enters Holland and is a free man Pat is welcomed into the Janus Venansius home where he is fed his first hot meal in seventy-two days.
November 21	Pat departs Rotterdam and arrives in London Pat sends telegram home to Momence announcing he is alive!
December 7	Pat meets privately with King George in Buckingham Palace

"In my hand I carried the stone in my handkerchief, and I made no effort to disguise its presence or its mission."

to the door. They couldn't speak English, and I could not speak Flemish, but I pointed to my flying-coat and then to the sky, and said "Fleger" ("Flyer"), which I thought would tell them what I was.

Whether they understood me or were intimidated by my hard-looking appearance I don't know, but certainly it would have to be a very brave man and boy who would start an argument with such a villainous-looking character as stood before them that night! I had not shaved for a month, my clothes were torn and dirty, my leggings were gone—they had got so heavy I had discarded them—my hair was matted, and my cheeks were flushed with fever. In my hand I carried the stone in my handkerchief, and I made no effort to disguise its presence or its mission.

They motioned me indoors and gave me the first hot meal I had had for a month. True, it consisted only of a few warm potatoes, but the old woman warmed them up in milk in one of the dirtiest kettles I had ever seen. I asked for bread, but she shook her head, although

Part VI

Home Again

Chapter Reference

PART VI ~ Home Again

Corresponding Chapters in "Lt. Pat O'Brien"	
Chapter 33 Atlantic Crossing	389
Chapter 34 Buck's Hunt	402
Chapter 35 Home at Last	416
Chapter 36 First Days Home	426
Chapter 37 First Tour	439
Chapter 38 Hatred for the Hun	454

Home Again ~ One can only imagine the thrill it was to see Pat step off the C&EI train at Momence on January 22, 1918. Three thousand men, women and children greeted him at the train station despite two feet of snow that had fallen in the area the day before. All Margaret could do was cry and say, "My big, big boy."

The next week was filled with reunions, a parade through town in the snow, a huge banquet at Wennerholm's Livery and a dance late into the morning at the south side dance hall. Pat had a week before his first formal speech at Orchestra Hall in Chicago. He spoke at a large reception in Lowell and gave three speeches in Kankakee. State officials attended and the press from around the country found the little town of Momence.

Pat's newly signed manager Lee Keedick saw the February 17 speech at Carnegie Hall as the true launch of Pat's national fame. Even in 1918, New York City was the center of communications and Keedick understood how to use the newspapers to promote his acts. The ripple effect of a story as dynamic as Pat O'Brien's would spread across the U.S. and all over free Europe in a matter of days. In one mouth's time, Pat became a household name, his book "Outwitting the Hun," would become a best seller and he would replace William Jennings Bryan as the most sought after and highest paid speaker in 1918. By the end of the year, Pat would begin to feel the tug of the war again and want to return. His health would eventually keep him home and his life would begin to change in 1919.

Reunion ~ Pat O'Brien with his brothers and Momence dignitaries the moment Pat step off the train at LaSalle Street Station in Chicago. Pat's brother Merwin "Buck" O'Brien (with Pat's suit case) spent three days and two trips trying to hook up with his brother. Unlike today, news of the arrival of his ship from England was premature and Buck returned from Toronto the first time having not found Pat but he was reunited with his brother on the second try.

To Pat's left is James Kirby, Edwin Chatfield, and James Cleary, known to have greeted Pat on the part of Momence. (specific identity of each not known) Pat's brother Perry is on the far right. The man looking down at Pat's trunk is believed to be Pat's brother Clarence. Note the London sticker on Pat's suitcase.

CHICAGO DAILY TRIBUNE
Friday, January 23, 1918

Momence Fetes Its Hero Song
Aviator "Pat" - Back from War
By Charles V. Julian

Momence, Illinois Jan. 22—(Special) Scalpers could have reaped a harvest here tonight when Momence feted its hero son, Lieut. Pat O'Brien of his majesty's flying corps. As high as $20 was offered for seats at the banquet for the hastily improvised auditorium in a local garage, but here are no dollar patriots in Momence, which boasts 103 stars in its service flag. Not a ticket changed hands for a monetary consideration.

Four hundred and fifty were seated at the banquet and 3,000 wished to attend to hear Mayor L. J. Tiffany greet the idol of all Kankakee county and to drink in the congratulation extended by Henry R. Rathbone, former president of the Hamilton club of Chicago, and the Rev. Father Bergen of St. Viator's college. Judge Landis and Lieut. Gov. Oglesby were unable to be present. Should some local historian ever attempt to set down the history of this little town on the banks of the Kankakee its alpha and omega will have chiefly to do with the amazing peregrinations of Happy Go Lucky Pat O'Brien.

Making the Most of It.

To call its very own a fighting man whose spectacular escape from a speeding train and whose subsequent flight through Germany thrilled two continents comes to most towns never, and this little city of Illinois is making the most of the occasion.

Momence never really expected it of Pat; little Pat who carried water for Contractor Clark when he build the brick building on Front street; mischievous Pat who was a lovable trial to his grade school teachers; Pat who didn't have time to bother much with high school books; Pat who at 15 contracted wanderlust.

Momence always knew that Pat would amount to something someday, for it's he a broth of an Irish lad with a way with colleen and a manner respected of gentlemen? And doesn't he come of the Fighting O'Briens and didn't he have a father and grandfather and a great-grandfather who fought side by side throughout the civil war in the famous One Hundred and Thirteenth Illinois? With that ancestry and his own cool daring Momence has always counted on Pat.

Too Much for Momence.

But that a son of this little island town in the marshlands of the Kankakee should startle a sensation sated world, should be entertained by the ruler of a mighty empire and be lionized in London, New York and Chicago—well, that is almost too much for Momence to fully comprehend.

But the town rose nobly to the occasion. All Momence was at the train. Schools were closed and many of the stores. Banners and flags of the allies lined the streets from the depot to the O'Brien home.
Pat—he refuses to be called by any other name—stepped from the train to face a brass band and a throng of people who had gathered from twenty miles around and to be clasped in a mother's arms.

"Hello, Mom"

"Hello, Mom," was his cheery greeting, but hers was only a sob as she reached up and softly touched the scars where a German bullet had harmed this six-foot giant who was still her boy.

"O, I'm all right now, mother," was his hasty reassurance as he turned with a shout to greet his brother. "Hello, Mulligan."

Mulligan's real name is Ivan and Brothers "Buck" and "Bud" are Merwin and Clarence in the family Bible. Then there are Brother Perry and sisters, Mrs. Clara Clegg and Mrs. Lila Worley, and Uncle Jeff on the G.A.R the proudest man in town; all the envy of Momence.

The girls! It's really too bad there aren't 300 Pats with cocky aviation hats that he might go around. Feminine Momence might then be satisfied. As it is, it's just, "Hello, Pat."

The call of the river where O'Brien spent many hours as a boy was too strong for the returned soldier to resist, and in the afternoon Pat doffed his uniform and put on a suit of his brother's clothes. Thus disguised, he slipped away from the crowds and for two hours had the time of his life skating on the old Kankakee.

A Welcome Home like no other ~Rare actual photo of Pat O'Brien amid his friends, family and citizens of Momence, Illinois on the day he arrived home. This photo appeared in the Momence *Progress* newspaper and was found on microfilm at the Chipman Public Library in Momence. Note Pat in the center of the crowd with marked by the white arrow. Margaret stands just behind him off his left shoulder. **Below**: Pat greets his mother, escorted by Clay Buntain to Majestic Theater in Kankakee for speech and at the Chicago train station. He was noticeably thin and weak from his ordeal.

Lowell, Indian Theatre where Pat spoke. Photo with plane and resulting prmotional poster plus appearance in San Francisco all in 1918.

Carnegie Hall~ Actual photo, taken from glass negative, of marquis outside Carnegie Hall showing Pat's first of two performances March 17, 1918

Greek Theatre
on Berkley Campus

Polis Theatre
Scranton, Pennsylvania

Municipal Auditorium
Oakland, California

Poli Theatre
Bridgeport,
Connecticut

Known Speeches by Pat O'Brien

DATE	DAY	Sponsor	YEAR	CITY	STA	LOCATION
January 23, 1918	Wednesday	Private	1918	Momence	IL	Livery building
January 24, 1918	Thursday	Elks Club	1918	Kankakee	IL	Elks Club - Kankakee
January 24, 1918	Thursday	Presbyrterian Church	1918	Kankakee	IL	Presbyrterian Church
January 24, 1918	Thursday	Rotary Club	1918	Kankakee	IL	McBroom Café
January 24, 1918	Thursday	Kankakee Woman's Club	1918	Kankakee	IL	Majestic Theatre
January 24, 1918	Thursday	Private	1918	Kankakee	IL	Majestic Theatre
January 25, 1918	Friday	Private	1918	Lowell	IN	Grand Theatre
January 28, 1918	Monday	St Patrick School	1918	Momence	IL	St Patrick School
January 29, 1918	Tuesday	Central School	1918	Momence	IL	Central School
February 1, 1918	Friday	Lee Keedick	1918	Chicago	IL	Orchestra Hall
February 3, 1918	Sunday	Private Diner	1918	Chicago	IL	Windermere Hotel
February 6, 1918	Wednesday	Lee Keedick	1918	Chicago	IL	Orchestra Hall
February 7, 1918	Thursday	Lee Keedick	1918	St. Louis	MO	Odean Hall
February 8, 1918	Friday	Unknown	1918	Peoria	IL	Uncertain
February 14, 1918	Thursday	Private	1918	Chicago	IL	Masonic Temple
February 17, 1918	Sunday	Lee Keedick	1918	New York	NY	Per New York Tmes
February 18, 1918	Monday (Est. Date!)	Lee Keedick	1918	Rochester	NY	Uncertain
February 21, 1918	Wednesday (Est. Date!)	Lee Keedick	1918	Trenton	NJ	Fort Dix
February 24, 1918	Sunday	Lee Keedick	1918	Philadelpia	PA	Academy of Music
March 10, 1918	Sunday	Lee Keedick	1918	Springfield	MA	YMCA Auditorium
March 19, 1918	Tuesday	Lee Keedick	1918	Boston	MA	Emerson Hall - Harvard University
March 20, 1918	Wednesday	Lee Keedick	1918	Providence	RI	Infantry Hall
March 21, 1918	Thursday	Lee Keedick	1918	Wilkes Barre	PA	Irem Temple
March 22, 1918	Friday	Interview	1918	Chicago	IL	Trains Station
March 23, 1918	Saturday	Interview	1918	Chicago	IL	Trains Station
March 23, 1918	Saturday	Lee Keedick	1918	Indianapolis	IN	All Souls Unitarian Church
March 24, 1918	Sunday	Lee Keedick	1918	Indianapolis	IN	Murat Theater
March 27, 1918	Wednesday	Interview	1918	Chicago	IL	As reported in Lima OH paper
March 29, 1918	Friday	Lee Keedick	1918	Minneapolis	MN	Location?
March 30, 1918	Saturday	Lee Keedick	1918	East		Story Says Pat went back east from Minneapolis
April 8, 1918	Monday	Lee Keedick	1918	Harrisburg	PA	Chestnut Street Auditorium
April 19, 1918	Not known	Lee Keedick	1918	Portland	OR	Article April 10, 1918 - said was there 3 weeks - Liberty L
April 20, 1918	Saturday	Lee Keedick	1918	Poughkeepsie	NY	Colingwood Opera House
April 21, 1918	Sunday	Lee Keedick	1918	DuBois	PA	Unknown
April 25, 1918	Thursday	Lee Keedick	1918	Baltimore	MD	Lyric of Baltimore
April 30, 1918	Tuesday	Not known	1918	Decatur	IL	Unknown
May 21, 1918	Tuesday	Lee Keedick	1918	Bridgeport	CT	Poli Theater
May 21, 1918	Tuesday	Lee Keedick	1918	Bridgeport	CT	Poli Theater
May 23, 1918	Thursday	Lee Keedick	1918	Washington	DC	New National Theater
May 23, 1918	Thursday	Lee Keedick	1918	Washington	DC	New National Theater
May 23, 1918	Thursday	Lee Keedick	1918	Baltimore	MD	Lyric of Baltimore
June 1, 1918	Saturday	Keedick?	1918	Pueblo	CO	Centential Auditorium
June 4, 1918	Monday	?	1918	Colorado Springs	CO	News states he spoke but does not say where
June 6, 1918	Wednesday	?	1918	Oklahoma City	OK	May News story states "booked" - like due to location
June 11, 1918	Tuesday	Keedick?	1918	Fort Worth	TX	Chamber of Commerce
June 13, 1918	Thursday	Keedick?	1918	San Antonio	TX	Main Avenue High School
June 14, 1918	Friday	Military	1918	San Antonio	TX	Kelly Field
June 15, 1918	Saturday	Military	1918	Dallas	TX	Fort Dick
June 15, 1918	Saturday	Military	1918	Dallas	TX	Fort Dick
June 16, 1918	Sunday	Military ?	1918	Dallas	TX	Dallas Coliseum - State Fair Grounds
June 21, 1918	Friday	Paul Elder?	1918	Los Angeles	CA	Trinity Auditorium
July 2, 1918	Tuesday	Paul Elder	1918	San Fransisco	CA	Dreamland Rink
July 3, 1918	Wednesday	Paul Elder	1918	Oakland	CA	Oakland Auditorium
July 5, 1918	Friday	Paul Elder (est.)	1918	Berkely	CA	Hearst Creek Theatre
July 10, 1918	Wednesday	Masons	1918	Stockton	CA	Masonic Temple
July 27, 1918	Saturday	Chautauqua	1918	Freeport	IL	Chautauqua Tent
August 1, 1918	Thursday	Chautauqua	1918	Marysville	OH	Chautauqua Tent
August 4, 1918	Sunday	Chautauqua	1918	Piqua	IA	Chautauqua Tent
August 8, 1918	Thursday	Chautauqua	1918	Connersville	IN	Cautauqua Tent
August 14, 1918	Wednesday	Chautauqua	1918	Pana	IL	Chautauqua Tent - Kitchell Park
August 15, 1918	Thursday	Chautauqua	1918	Sullivan	IL	Chautauqua Tent - Seas Park
August 15, 1918	Thursday	Chautauqua	1918	Decatur	IL	Chautauqua Tent
September 15, 1918	Sunday	Greater I & I Fair	1918	Danville	IL	Chautaqua Tent
September 21, 1918	Saturday	Momence Bond Committee	1918	Momence	IL	Speaks at Liberty Bond rally
October 3, 1918	Thursday	Chautauqua	1918	Cedar Falls	IA	Iowa State Teachers College
October 4, 1918	Friday	Chautauqua	1918	Waterloo	IA	Waterloo Theatre
October 5, 1918	Saturday	Chautauqua	1918	Waterloo	IA	Auditorium at Cattle Congress
October 14, 1918	Monday	Chautauqua	1918	LaCrosse	WI	LaCrosse Theater
November 28, 1918	Thursday	Manteno Schools	1918	Manteno	IL	Manteno High School - Did not appear
February 5, 1919	Wednesday	Unknown	1919	Canton	OH	Municipal Auditorium
February 18, 1919	Tuesday	Amer Inst. Mining	1919	New York	NY	Biltmore Hotel
February 24, 1919	Monday	Unknown - Booking Agent	1919	New York	NY	Palace Theater
March 9, 1919	Sunday (Est. Date!)	B.F. Keith	1919	New York	NY	B.F. Keith's Vaudville Theater
April 4, 1919	Monday	Unknown	1919	Chicago	IL	Majestic Theatre

LIEUT. PAT O'BRIEN STIRS LOCAL AUDIENCE WITH STORY

He belongs to the Royal Flying corps of Great Britain, this young lieutenant, "Pat" O'Brien, with the black, wiry, stiff hair standing up like bristles all over his head, and the tragedy of the pitiless world war in his young face, a face that smiles brightly, but is still pallid from the pain of terrible wounds and the misery of the Hun prison camp. He belongs to the Royal Flying corps, this muscular youth with the Irish name. But when a Chieftain reporter asked him right off the bat what part of England he called home, he looked surprised and said with just the right touch of pride in his tone, "Oh, I'm from Illinois, Momence, Ill."

Sure, Pat O'Brien is an Irish-American, or an American Irishman. He is one of those many heroes of the British flying corps whose American sense of right was so stirred by the stories of outrages which accompanied the first charge of the Huns into defenseless Belgium, that they threw their courage and their fortunes into the side of the allies, left happy homes and prosperity in America, and went across to help stop the hordes from the Baltic caves.

Of all the heroes who have pitted their skill as aviators against the Germans, Pat O'Brien has perhaps suffered most and lived to tell his story. Shot down inside the British lines, shot down in No Man's land, and shot down inside the German lines, wounded, made prisoner, hunted like a criminal across a nation where every human creature was arrayed against him, Pat O'Brien is not whipped yet. He is going back just as soon as his legs get a bit steadier, the wound in his shoulder heals completely, and his stiff fingers become limber enough to hold true the rudder of an aeroplane. He is going back because he realizes that somebody has got to whip the Germans if civilization and human liberty are to be preserved.

He is willing to do his bit, not because he loves being a target for trained men with long range anti-aircraft guns, not because he likes to kill a German aviator in a lonely duel above the clouds, but because he feels there is a battle raging in which right is imperiled by might. He goes back because he wants to give his strength and skill and life if need be, in the cause of right.

Lieutenant Pat O'Brien, when he straightens up to his full height, is around six feet tall. He is every inch an athlete and has the quick, keen athletic eye without which no man can succeed in any sort of athletics, and possessing which a man can go in for all sorts of sports. O'Brien's eye happens to be black, but it is more in the sparkle than the color that the eye of the athlete is noted. Before entering the war Lieutenant O'Brien was one of the greatest trick flyers in the world and his exhibition flights were sought everywhere. He was amassing a huge fortune when he decided that there was something in the world bigger than money and rushed to a Canadian recruiting office to enlist in the fight against the Huns at a salary which less for a year than he used to make in a day.

None of these facts O'Brien told in his address last night at Centennial auditorium before an audience that filled the place to seating capacity. He lectured on the war last night under the National League for Women's Service, founded for the purpose of aiding to win this war. In his style which has been made familiar to millions of Americans thru his popular book, he told his story of the war, of the battles in the clouds and on the grounds, of how it feels to be shot down, and how it feels to win over an opponent in a battle high in the heavens which is a battle to the death. He told of the misery of the prisoners taken by the Germans and of his famous escape and his long struggle to reach the British line again.

One of the points brought out by O'Brien was that the German is a "snake" in his war methods. That he will use anything from explosive bullets to a stab in the back. "I have heard the peculiar sizzling of an explosive bullet, just before it bursts, many a time as they plunged into some part of my aeroplane, and have heard them burst before they strike sometimes. They are terrible for the awful wounds they make, crippling for life when they do not kill and making miserable sores which torment the wounded as long as they live, instilling a slow poison into the system."

O'Brien's fingers are mishapen from dragging himself across the shell torn surface of No Man's land. His wound in the back of the shoulder was received in midair. He has been in almost daily combat except the time he spent as a prisoner of war, and left the British hospitals last December on an indefinite furlough in the hopes that a trip to his native land might prove beneficial.

Lieutenant O'Brien told his audience last night that all the tricks of aeroplaning that formerly were considered sheer daredeviltry are now absolutely necessary in air fighting, and the aviator capable of darting and swirling and gliding and dropping is in better position to protect his life and destroy enemy planes. He told of how diligently the aviators are now being trained in "stunts."

Lieutenan O'Brien thrilled his audience to unstinted applause. He arrived in Pueblo shortly after noon yesterday and was met at the depot by Floyd C. Tallmadge of this city, formerly of Momence, Ill., and a boyhood friend of Lieutenant O'Brien. Lieutenant O'Brien was a guest at the Tallmadge home on Greenwood street last night, and will leave on his lecture tour at 9 o'clock this morning.

The Carnegie Hall Speech

It was, as it turned out, Pat's firsthand experience with the Hun that made his claims so compelling and built passion for the Allied effort at Carnegie Hall. After concluding his one hour and thirty minute speech, Pat gave a heartfelt thank-you to the Carnegie Hall crowd and raising his cane overhead, paid a final farewell, "Good Night, folks!" They rose to their feet in thunderous applause.

Streams of reporters could be seen hunched over, rushing out of the famous venue to immediately file stories with their papers as the crowd screamed with delight. Keedick was ecstatic. He knew what rapidly exiting reporters meant. It was the fuse that would explode Pat O'Brien onto every front page in America. The next day he was proven right.

Philadelphia, Boston, Providence, Baltimore, Toronto, Cleveland, Chicago, Waterloo, Denver, Dallas, San Francisco, Los Angles, and even Calgary, Canada ran stories the next day about the new national hero, Lieutenant Pat O'Brien and his amazing story of escape and, of all things, his visit with the King.

from "Lt. Pat O'Brien"

Lieut. Pat O'Brien

Royal Flying Corps
AUTHOR OF
"Outwitting the Hun"

WILL DELIVER HIS THRILLING WAR LECTURE

"My Escape from a German Prison Camp"

One of the most remarkable stories of adventure yet recorded.
— Philadelphia Evening Ledger

He matched Yankee strategy against German efficiency and won.
— Chicago Examiner

Lieut. Pat O'Brien, who was captured by the Germans and subsequently escaped by jumping from a car window, told the story of that escape to an audience which crowded Carnegie Hall last night.
— New York Times

The most extraordinary personal experience of the war.
— Brooklyn Eagle

Pat O'Brien is an American war hero of the first water.
— New York Sun

Lieutenant Pat O'Brien, American, though a member of the Royal Flying Corps, needed no moving pictures to enthrall an audience that crowded the Academy of Music last night.
— Philadelphia Ledger

He had an audience with him right then and there; he had captured them just as he had the Hun birdman with the sure shots fired from his machine thousands of feet in the air. There is nothing like it and probably nothing ever will be like it. Each day is a volume. Yes, each minute is an eternity.
— Pittsburg Post

At the Cotton Palace Coliseum
Wednesday Evening, June 12th

Lieutenant O'Brien belongs to the class of heroes who acquire that distinction by individual acts of bravery in the face of imminent danger of personal injury and death, and as such his name will be read in history with the other names made famous by deeds of daring and death-defying courage.

Rendered unconscious by a bullet wound at an altitude of over 8000 feet, he crashed down to earth, and lived. Captured by the Germans, he was being transported to a reprisal prison camp, when he leaped through the window of a speeding express train and escaped in the darkness.

Then began his marvelous journey through Germany, Luxemburg and Belgium, 250 miles, 72 days, 30 days in the uniform of a British officer, which ended when he dug his way beneath an electric fence and knelt upon the soil of Holland to thank God for his deliverance.

General Admission 30c; Reserved Seats 55c; Box Seats $1.10

SEATS ON SALE AT POWERS-KELLY DRUG CO., FIFTH AND AUSTIN STREETS.

Part VII

Elusive Journey

Chapter Reference

PART VII ~ Elusive Journey

Corresponding Chapters in "Lt. Pat O'Brien"	
Chapter 39 Reunions	471
Chapter 40 Agnes	488
Chapter 41 Return to France	504
Chapter 42 Pulling Away	518
Chapter 43 Conversations	535
Chapter 44 Precipitous Passing	557
Chapter 45 Shanghai	571
Chapter 46 Siberia	588
Chapter 47 Harry Tates	606
Chapter 48 The Bypass	623

OUTWITTING THE HUN
Lieut. PAT O'BRIEN

Elusive Journey ~ Looking back nearly 100 years, is hard to appreciate the impact of Pat O'Brien's book, "Outwitting the Hun," on the American public. When the war erupted in 1914, President Woodrow Wilson pledged neutrality, a position favored by the vast majority of Americans. But by the release of Pat's book in January, 1918, America had been in the war for nine months, the mood of the country had changed. The public could not get enough war news to satisfy their patriotic fervor.

"Outwitting the Hun" was an immediate best-seller and it was contemporary. After all, Pat's crash, survival and escape had occurred less than two months prior to its release. Excerpts were printed in nearly every newspaper in the country filling major concert halls and small town opera houses for nearly a year. Pat stirred the passions of everyone that heard him. He signed hundreds of books, raised millions in war bonds and became the best known war hero of 1918.

Within a week of his homecoming he was on a chase, first Chicago, then New York, Baltimore, Washington, St. Louis, Dallas and every major city in the United States. It was his story in "Outwitting the Hun," that caused him to go on a never-ending chase to the next city, caused a constant crush of admirers to chase after him in every town and propelled him past his family, his hometown, some much needed rest, and past the woman he loved, Agnes MacMillan.

By the end of the year, he'd had enough and began to chase after his unfinished war despite its sudden end and his unqualified state of health.

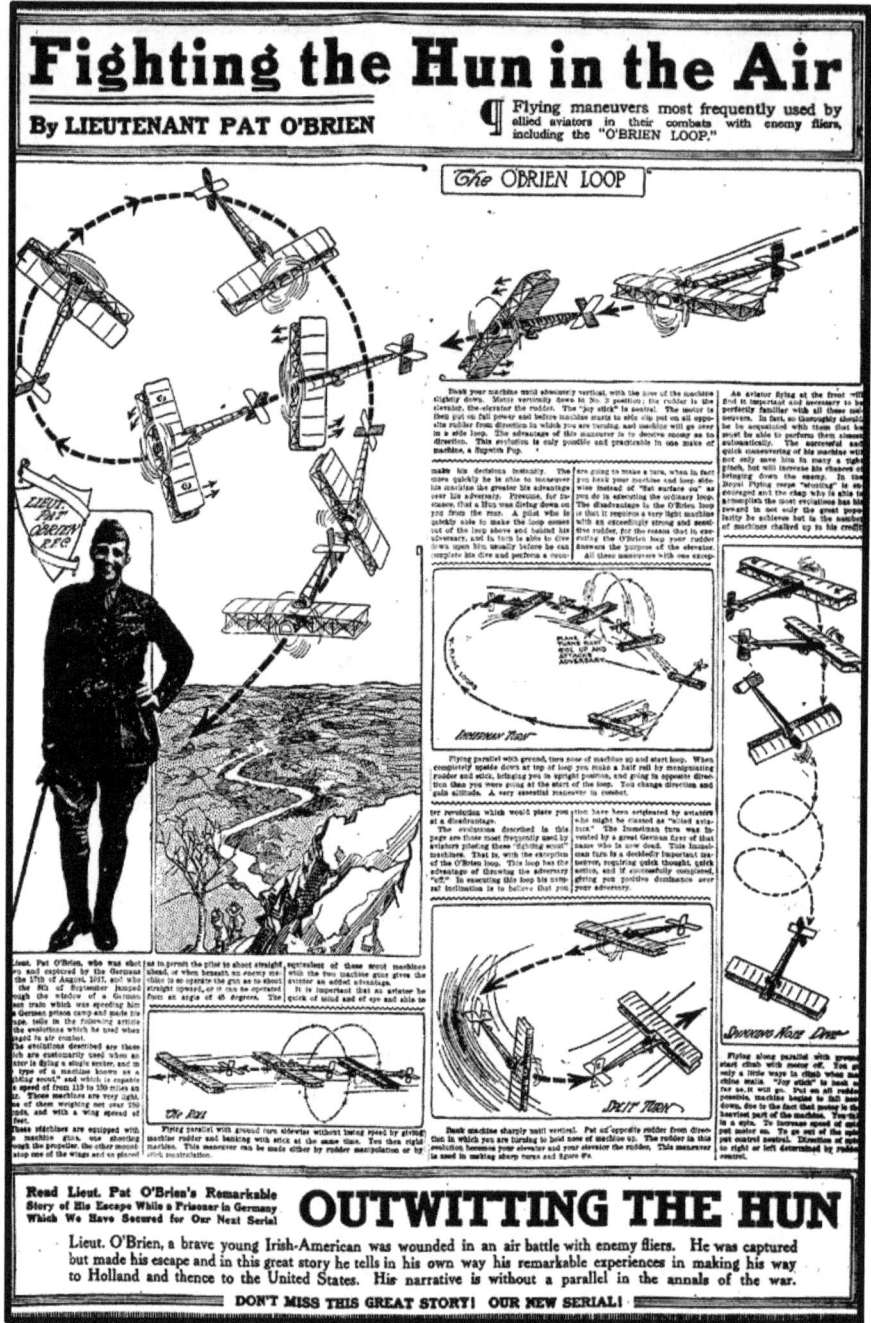

"The O'Brien Loop," proven to be true based on the research of these authors, was part of the folklore that grew throughout 1918 about Pat. The reality of Pat's experience was never overshadowed by fictitious tales of his

Lieut. Pat O'Brien, War Hero

HIS ADVICE TO THE AMERICAN BOYS WHO GO "OVER THERE" SHOWN IN SKETCHES

LIEUT. PAT O'BRIEN COMING

War Hero Will Tell Experiences in Oklahoma Next Month.

Special to The World

OKLAHOMA CITY, May 28.—Pat O'Brien has been secured for an address in Oklahoma City on June 6, when he will tell about his famous escape from German soldiers when he leaped from the train in which he was being taken to a German prison camp. Proceeds will go to the anti-tuberculosis fund.

Oklahoma City, Oklahoma

SAYS LIEUT. O'BRIEN'S IS BEST STORY OF WAR

Capt. Edwin Bower Hesser, late of the Photographic division, Aviation section, U. S. Signal Corps, is in town arranging the lecture appearance of Lieut. Pat O'Brien, the famous "ace" of the Royal Flying Corps who was shot down behind the lines of Germany and made a prisoner by the Huns. Lt. O'Brien is to lecture on "My Escape from a German Prison Camp," at the high school auditorium Tuesday evening, Feb. 18, according to Capt. Hesser's announcement.

San Antonio, Texas

PAT O'BRIEN ADMITS HIS GUILT OF PRANK

Berkeley, Calif., March 5.—A college prank which proved a mystery to the University of California for several years was cleared up here recently when Lieut. Pat O'Brien, the American ace, who fell 8,000 feet into Germany and then escaped from a Hun prison camp, confessed to an audience of 10,000 in the Hearst Greek theater that he was "guilty."

On a St. Patrick's day several years ago the university woke up to find its beautiful gold letter "C" on Charter Hill, overlooking the campus, shining forth in brilliant green. Investigations failed to disclose whose hand had redecorated the big "C" and the school officials never knew until Lieutenant O'Brien made his "confession."

Berkley, California

PROGRAM WILL BEGIN AT 8:30 O'CLOCK TO ACCOMODATE BUSINESS MEN

Owing to the great desire of many business men whose places of business remain open late on Saturday night, to attend, it has been decided to have Lieutenant Pat O'Brien begin his lecture at 8:30 o'clock tonight instead of at 8 o'clock as previously mentioned.

Pueblo, Colorado

Lieut. Pat O'Brien at the Palace.

Lieutenant Pat O'Brien, war hero and author of "Outwitting the Hun," made his first appearance in vaudeville yesterday afternoon at the Palace Theatre, entertaining the audience with an account of his war experiences. Ruth St. Denis returned to the Palace stage with a new dancing act, and the program also included Louise Dresser and Jack Gardner, George White, and Frank Fay.

The New York Times
Copyright © The New York Times
Originally published February 25, 1919

New York, New York

PROFITEERING ON HERO'S LECTURES CHARGED, DENIED

Charges that Leo Keedick of New York, manager for Lieut. Pat O'Brien on his lecture tours, had demanded half of the gross receipts should O'Brien lecture in Chicago at a benefit for the relief of Belgian prisoners in Germany, were characterized as "absurd" by Keedick when seen by a representative of THE TRIBUNE in New York last night.

Chicago, Illinois

> ## "Some Day I'll Stub My Toe, Fall Down and Break My Neck"
>
> That's What
>
> Smiling **PAT O'BRIEN** Lieut R. F. C.
>
> Said after being shot down 8,000 feet in the air behind German lines; taken prisoner, leaping through the window of a speeding express train and then his marvelous journey through Germany, Luxemburg and Belgium, 250 miles, 72 days, 30 days in the uniform of a British officer, digging his way beneath an electric fence into Holland, then coming to this country and falling 1000 feet, doing stunts for the movies at Reily Field.
>
> HEAR HIM GIVE HIS STARTLING LECTURE
>
> ## "MY ESCAPE FROM A GERMAN PRISON CAMP"
>
> ONE MINUTE HE THRILLS YOU—THE NEXT HE HAS YOU DOUBLED UP WITH LAUGHTER.
>
> APPEARING AT THE
>
> ## LA CROSSE THEATRE
>
> NEXT MONDAY, OCTOBER 14—MATINEE AT 2:30; NIGHT AT 8:15.
>
> PRICES: BALCONY 50c   LOWER FLOOR 75c   War Tax Additional   Seats Now Selling

From "Lt. Pat O'Brien" On the long train ride home, Pat told Elmer of his visit to Richmond, his engagement to Agnes and his plans to end touring after his Chautauqua tour. He also told him about his plans to go to France. He'd leave after his last speech scheduled for LaCrosse, Wisconsin on October 14th.

The La Crosse Tribune and Leader Press ad read, "One minute he thrills you – the next he has you doubled up with laughter." The description was true and had certainly been so since Pat first spoke to the Troops in London three days after his escape. What was different now was how Pat was being "sold."

No one in La Crosse or the rest of the country knew that the war would end in exactly four weeks. But Pat's promoters had sensed over the summer that selling Pat O'Brien on patriotism alone might not stir enough interest, even in La Crosse, Wisconsin. They understood that suspense and humor had to replace the fervent patriotism once used as the primary draw for Pat O'Brien. Pat understood this before anyone else.

"So They Could Not Trail Me By My Blood"

YOU Americans who want to know how a plain young Chicago boy can play tricks with the German army, read this true tale by Lieutenant Pat O'Brien. The Hun couldn't hold him—this young daredevil American boy. How will they hold those others—those millions like Pat O'Brien who are now "over there" or on their way?

This is what Pat O'Brien did—or part of it. He fell in his aeroplane 8,000 feet into the German lines. He was nearly dead, but they couldn't kill him. They started him on the way to prison. All they had to hold him was a train going 35 miles an hour and four armed guards. But that couldn't hold our young man. He leaped from the window of the flying train.

Then for 72 days he ran and hid and crawled and swam and cajoled and fought—through Luxembourg—through Belgium—to—but read the story yourself.

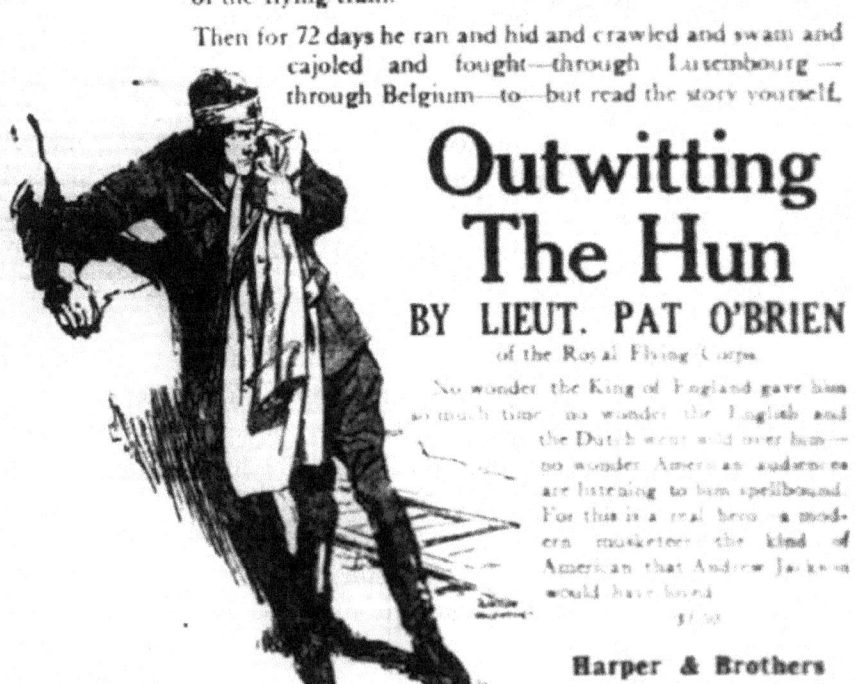

Outwitting The Hun

BY LIEUT. PAT O'BRIEN
of the Royal Flying Corps

No wonder the King of England gave him so much time—no wonder the English and the Dutch went wild over him— no wonder American audiences are listening to him spellbound. For this is a real hero—a modern musketeer—the kind of American that Andrew Jackson would have loved.

$1.50

Harper & Brothers
ESTABLISHED 1817

New York Times, April 7, 1918

The Huns couldn't hold him!

FROM 8,000 feet in the air he had swirled down into their camp, wounded, helpless. They thought him dead— but they little knew the indomitable soul that lived in this Irish-American — the soul that laughed at things that would have killed another man.

THEIR train was rushing him to the prison camp at 45 miles an hour. He was wounded, shaky, sick. The German guard sat beside him with gun loaded and ready to shoot. And from this he escaped.

It was 72 days before he was safe—72 days of crawling and slipping by night and hiding by day—bleeding, wounded— passing sentries boldly—fighting peasants—winding up in that dramatic crossing of the barbed wire fence that Germany considers so sure a boundary line.

NO wonder he was received with joy by the English public—no wonder audiences listen breathlessly to his story all over the United States. YOU can read it now, for he has told it in his new book. This long-limbed, hawk-faced, daredevil son of Chicago—they could not keep him out of the war—they could not kill him—they could not hold him! Read this story at once. Get his book at your bookseller's. It is a great story of that indomitable spirit that makes America unconquerable, invincible.

Outwitting the Hun

By Lt. PAT O'BRIEN, Royal Flying Corps.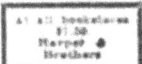

A Glorious Tale of 72 Days' Escaping from Germany

New York Times, March 4, 1918

"Lt. Pat O'Brien" Timeline

May 19, 1918 - May 6, 1919

May 19	Pat speaks at National Theatre in Washington, D.C.
June 1	Pat speaks in Pueblo, Colorado
June 8	Pat speaks in Oklahoma City, Oklahoma
June 13	Pat speaks in San Antonio, Texas
June 14	Pat speaks to troops in Dallas, Texas Pat crashes demonstration airplane and survives
June 25	Pat back in San Francisco. Sees Agnes
August 15	Pat speaks in Sullivan, Illinois. Sarah Otis attends with friends. Visits Pat and his brother
September 21	Pat visits his mother in Lowell. She is sick.
October 14	Pat's final Chautauqua speech in La Crosse, Wisconsin
October 25	Pat leaves for France. Plans to join Legion
November 11	War ends in Europe
December 10	Pat back in U.S.
March 22	Agnes gives birth to Pat's child Carol
May 8	Al Fontaine returns from War. He and Pat visit.

May 19	Pat and his mother depart for Wyoming and family reunion with the Hathaways
May 25	Pat says, "good bye" to the Hathaways for the last time.
May 26	Pat spends final time with Agnes in San Francisco
May 30	Pat boards ship in Seattle for Russia
June 26	Pat in Yokohama, Japan
June 28	Pat arrives in Shanghai, China
June 11	Pat arrives in Tianjin, China
August 15	Agnes gives Carol to George and Vesta Hughes who will raise her. It is decided that Agnes will be in Carol's life. She will be referred to as "Aunt Agnes." Pat was never told he had a daughter.
August 18	Pat in Peking, China (approximate date)
August 23	Pat in Vladivostok, Russia
August 25	Pat boards Trans-Siberian Railroad train for inner Russia (approximate date)
September 3	Pat abandons train, head South through the Daijing Gate at Zhangjiakou in the Great Wall.
October 5	Pat back in Yokohama
October 26	Pat back in the United States, arrives in Seattle

Who was Agnes MacMillan? ~ No one in Momence, including the O'Brien family nor anyone except her descendants in Nevada, knew who Agnes MacMillan was when "Finding Pat O'Brien" began in 2007. And yet, Agnes was the most important person in the life of Pat O'Brien. Without her story, the story the true identity of Pat O'Brien would include a gaping hole and leave his legacy even more nebulous than it is today.

Pat met Agnes sometime in late in 1914 or early 1915. No one alive today knows the date for certain. Pat had just moved to Richmond, California and had a job with the Santa Fe Railroad. Being the terminus for the Transcontinental Railroad, Richmond was a logical place for Pat as a result of his love of trains begun as a young lad in Momence. Agnes was a strong, independent beautiful woman of Scottish decent. She worked at the fashionable City of Paris Store in San Francisco and possessed an equal amount of flair and style that was very much of a part of San Francisco from the beginning. To Pat, she was a balance of strength, beauty and grace and equal to him and at her core, likely stronger than he. We speculate that Agnes understood intuitively the complete Pat O'Brien, brazen, daring and charming on the outside yet simple, genuine and vulnerable inside.

Four years into the "Finding Pat O'Brien" project, the authors were introduced to Agnes MacMillan by her two granddaughters who were also seeking to "find" Pat O'Brien, their grandfather. Once we knew of Agnes, we knew much more about Pat and the search extended for two more years until the publication of "Lt. Pat O'Brien" in 2013.

And finally, Kevin McNulty met Leslie Jacobs and Lori Floto on July 22. 2014 in Reno, Nevada. The story of their mother Carol, the child of Agnes MacMillan and Pat O'Brien, is revealed for the first time in this book. As of this time, no photo of Agnes has been found but McNulty believes it is likely in the months ahead. Leslie and Lori also have a brother, Jon, Pat's grandson.

In the years ahead, the authors hope that more is learned about Agnes. Both Leslie, Lori and Jon referred to Agnes all their lives as "Aunt Agnes." Their mother, the baby of Pat and Agnes, was raised by George and Vesta Hughes of San Bruno, California from her very earliest days. Agnes knew her grandchildren and they knew her. Based on our research and the opinion of Leslie and Lori, only one person did not know about the baby Carol - Pat O'Brien, himself.

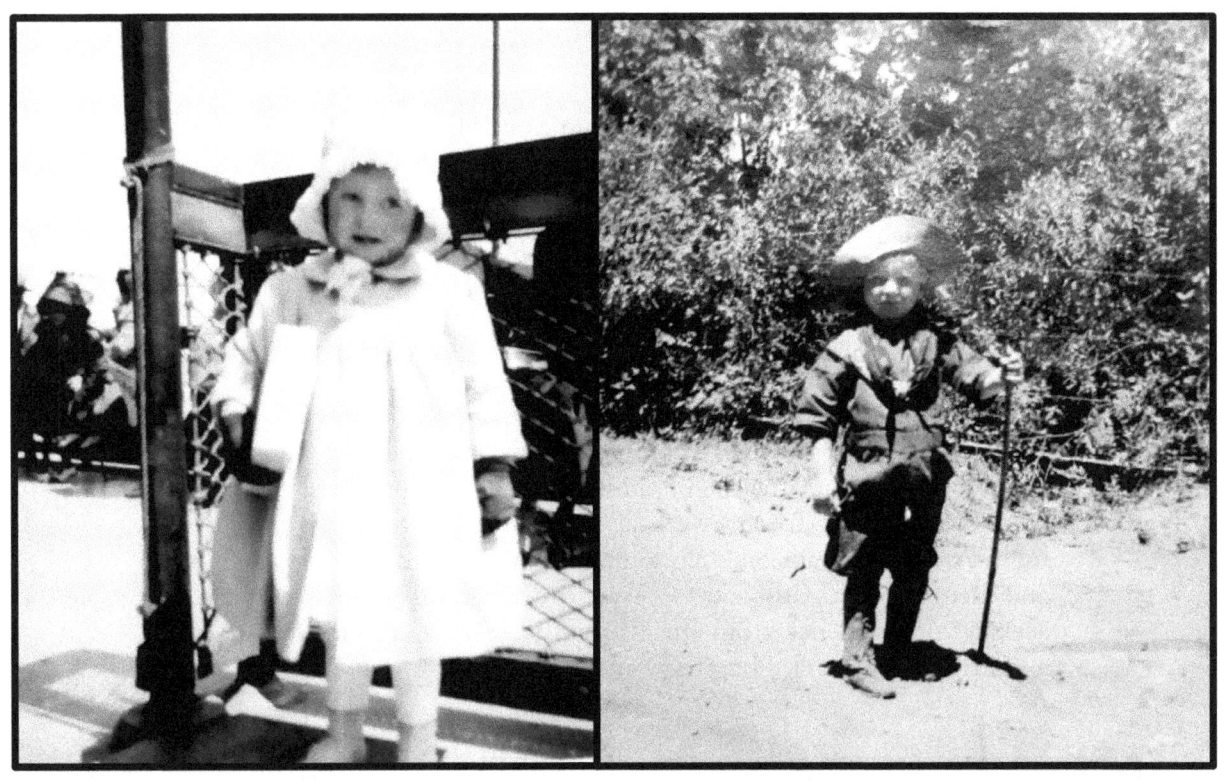

Carol Ruth (O'Brien) Hughes (above)
George Hughes - Vesta Hughes and Carol Ruth (below)

Russia ~ The next morning Pat was up early. His train pulled out of the Mukden station at 6:00 a.m. and headed straight north to the city of Harbin where he transferred to the Trans-Manchurian railroad and headed straight east toward Vladivostok, Russia. He had been advised to enter the city using this route as opposed to the Trans-Siberian Railroad which lay a bit farther north. "You can sneak into town a bit easier this way," the Australian Colonel had told him.

Pat was not the only person attempting to "sneak" into Vladivostok during the summer of 1919. Thousands of civilians, military, industrialists, former government officials, businessmen, railroad operators, and 60,000 crack Czech-Slavic troops were all attempting to travel five-thousand miles across the Trans-Siberian Railway to Vladivostok unnoticed. White and Red loyalists, Cossacks, thieves and disgruntled political factions seeking independence from the Russian state were all picking off men and materiel of any ilk along the way.

PAT O'BRIEN'S TRIP TO RUSSIA/CHINA/JAPAN
Carol Ruth (O'Brien) Hughes is born as Pat heads for Russia

> Carol was born March 21, 1919. Pat had spoken to Agnes on the phone but had not seen her during her pregnancy due to his time in France, attempting to join the French foreign Legion. He returns to the United States and announces his plans to travel to Russia where 40,000 Czech troops are trapped in Siberia amid the Russian civil war. Agnes chooses not to tell Pat about the baby. She wishes to know if he will marry her without knowledge of the child. She still wears Pat's engagement ring given to her months ago. Pat announces he's leaving and Agnes decides that they will have no future together. Neither Agnes nor Pat knows that they will never see each other again. Pat dies not knowing he is a father to Carol.

MARCH
March 21 — Carol (Agnes' baby) is born

MAY
May 13 — Pat gets passport in Chicago – Permit to China -
May 30 — Pat boards train in Richmond for Seattle

JUNE
June 2 — Pat's Passport signed in Seattle – permit to sail
June 7 — Pat's passport signed to sail on "The Empress of Russia"
Pat departs Vancouver for Yokohama on "The Empress of Russia"
June 19 — Pat arrives in Yokohama
June 28 — Pat's Steamer arrives in Shanghai from Yokohama

JULY
July 1 — Russian Embassy in Shanghai signs Pat's Passport for trip to Russia
July 7 — British Counsel General in Shanghai signs Pat passport permit for Vladivostok, Omsk via Mukden

AUGUST
August 11 — Pat leaves Shanghai for Tianjin
August 14 — Pat arrives in Tianjin
August 18 — Pat goes to Peking
August 16 — Agnes gives up Carol to George and Vesta Hughes (approximate)
August 19 — American Consulate signs Pat's passport in Peking – permission to China, Russian, Japan

Pat O'Brien Is Going to Fight Siberian Bosheviks

Far into the interior of Siberia, where railroads and ships are unheard of, there is an army of unknown quantity waging war with the Bolsheviki. But America's Pat O'Brien, famous aviator, heard about this army. It is made up of Chinese, Manchurians, Koreans, Japanese, et al, but no Americans. Pat O'Brien is

Pat's final "battle" is along the Trans-Siberian Railroad where he comes to peace with the loss of Paul Raney and his own valid contribution tot he War.

PAT O'BRIEN WILL TOUR ABROAD.

Lieut. Pat O'Brien who has been a guest of Mrs. Clara Clegg and Mrs. Margaret O'Brien for several days, went to Chicago Monday; from there he will go to New York city, on a business trip; he will then return to Momence and in company with his mother they will make a visit with relatives at different points in Wyoming, leaving here the latter part of May. Pat will then go to Vancover, British Columbia, where on June the 12th he will sail on the wonderful ship "The Empress of Russia" and will spend sometime touring Japan, China, and Siberia. He expects to be absent six months and possibly will not return for a couple of years.

PAT'S PASSPORT PHOTO FOR TRIP TO RUSSIA/CHINA

(The following are estimated dates by the authors. Passport dates are accurate)

August 20	Pat checks out of Peking hotel to head back to Tianjin
August 21	Pat travels to Mukden from Tianjin – 8 hours
August 22	Pat departs Mukden for Vladivostok 8 hours – arrives that night
August 24	Pat visits the Red Cross in Vladivostok
August 25	Pat departs Vladivostok for Khabarovsk – stops then travels after sundown
August 26	Travel day – full day
	Stop at – Rukhlovo/Two ambushes
August 28	Harry Tate Aircraft – Pat Flies – stays overnight in Slyvynka
August 29	Pat heads for Urga
August 30	Pat heads south from Urga into Gobi Desert
August 31	Travel on the Gobi

SEPTEMBER

September 1 (Mon)	Travel on the Gobi
September 2 (Tues)	Travel on the Gobi
September 3 (Wed)	Travel on the Gobi
September 4 (Thur)	Travel on the Gobi

OCTOBER

October 6	American Embassy's signs Pat's Passport in Yokohama to return home.
October 24 (Fri)	Pat arrives back in Seattle "S.S. Fushimi Mura"

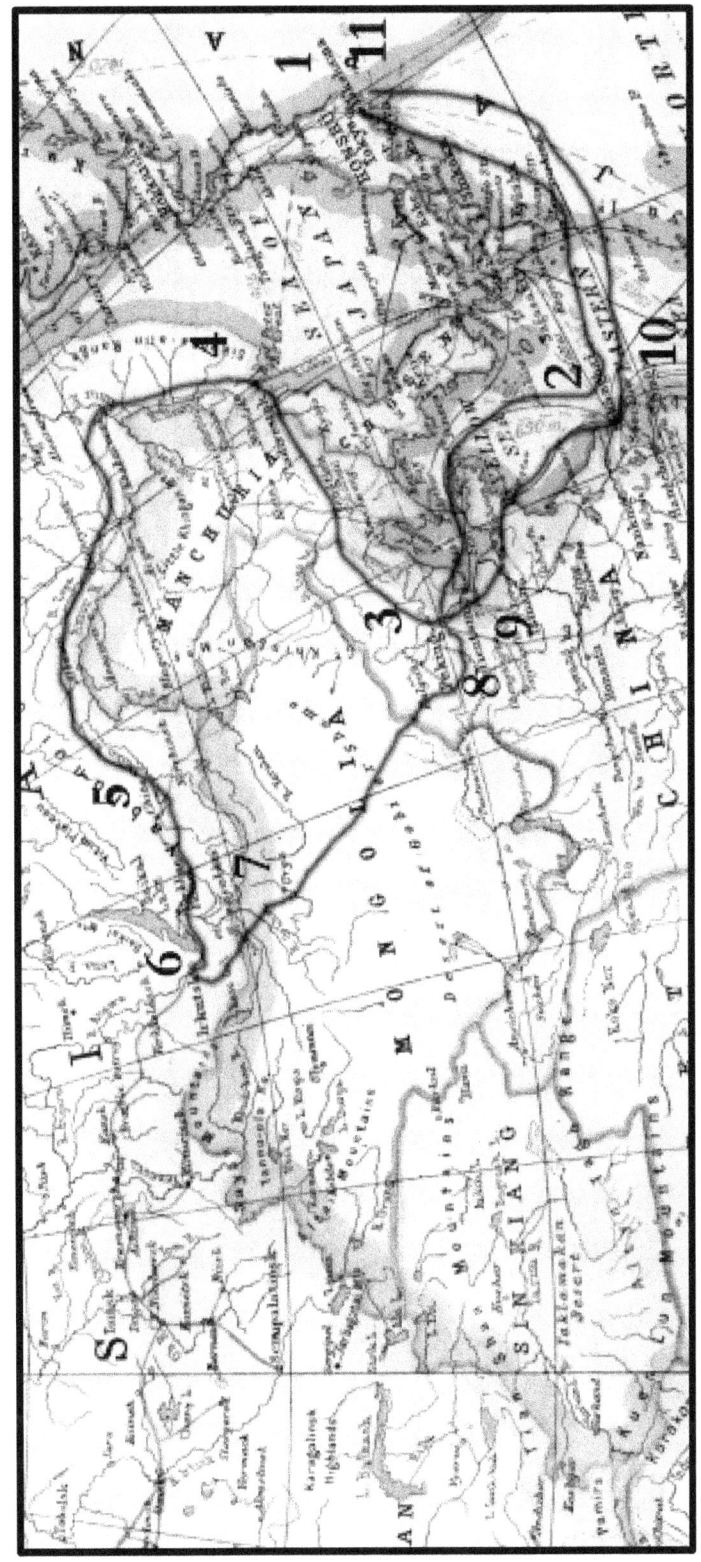

Pat's Route - Japan/China/Russia May 30, 1919 to October 26, 1919

Seattle - (May 30)

1. Yokohama - (June 26)

2. Shanghai - (June 28)

3. Tianjian & Peking, China -(June 30)

4. Vladivostok, Russia (August 23)

5. Chita, Russia (est. August 28)

6. Slyudyankaf, Russia (est. August 30)

7. Urga Mongolia (est. August 31)

8. Peking, China (est. Sept 5)

9. Tianjian, China (est. Sept 7)

10. Shanghai, China (est. Sept 9)

11. Yokohama, Japan (Oct 5)

Seattle (October 26)

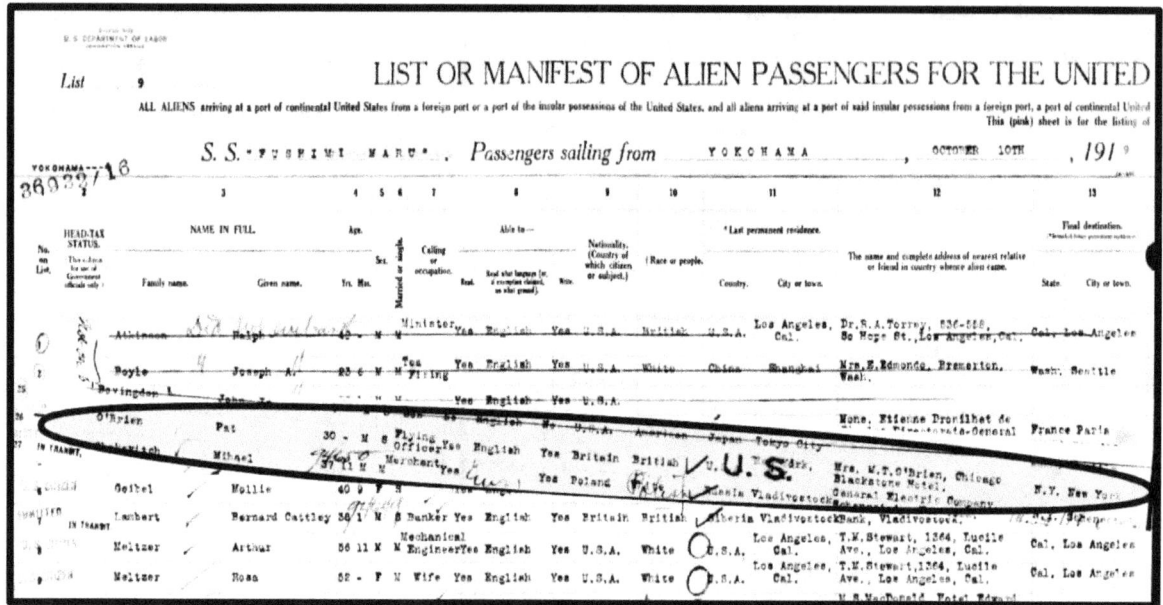

Ship's Manifest - Shows Pat aboard the S.S. Fushimi Maru departing Yokohama for Seattle on October 10, 1919, heading home from Asian trip to an America that is changing rapidly.

The Allen Car - Photo of the Allen Car similar to the one used by Pat to cross the Gobi Desert. He likes the care so much he purchased an Allen Car dealership in Los Angeles during 1920. The business failed mostly due to lack of support from the manufacturer who was simply shedding inventory and

The Astor Hotel, Pat's hotel in Shanghai in 1919

The Bund in Yokohama where Pat visited on his way to Russia

The scene in Vladivostok when Pat arrived. Hundreds of Allied troops including U.S., Canadian, British, Japanize and others entered Russia to free 40,000 Czech troops from the chaos of the Russian Revolution. It was here that Pat observed the opportunistic Japanize, leading him to pursue "Shadows of the West," an anti-Japanize film that foresaw the threat realized on December 7, 1941. Below: the streets of Vladivostok upon Pat's

The Japanese Threat

War in Western Europe had ended by late 1918. But in Russia, there was a situation that took precedent over any post-war manipulation of the Europeans map. Vladimir Lennon had taken over Moscow and most Russian cities in western Russia, causing thousands of loyal Tsarist armies to flee east to Vladivostok and the Pacific Coast. Basically, the Triple Entente countries of Britain, France and Tsarist Russia, along with 40,000 Czechoslovakian troops were trapped in the crossfire. America and the Japanese agreed to help, sending 7,000 troops each. In no time, Japan had increased their presence to 72,000 troops.

It did not take long for American troops to notice that the Japanese were not just interested in "helping out." After all, they had shown their aggression in the Russo-Japanese War of 1905. Pat O'Brien and every American that witnessed the aggressive nature of the Japanese in Vladivostok and surrounding areas knew that Japan would be the next imperial threat to the world.

Had Pat not gone to Russia, he would have never witnessed the Japanese threat first hand. Until Vladivostok, the Hun was the bane of Pat O'Brien. After Russian, he knew Japan could be an equal threat. Little did he know that in a twenty short years, both would turn the world inside out once again. So concerned was the newly formed American Legion that they included the filming of "Shadows of the West" as one of their first projects. They would cast the most popular war hero of the time in their anti-Japanese film, none other than Lt. Pat O'Brien.

124

Part VIII
Downward Spiral

Chapter Reference

PART VIII ~ Downward Spiral

Corresponding Chapters in "Lt. Pat O'Brien"

Chapter 49	McGraw	645
Chapter 50	Whirlwind	665
Chapter 51	The Swarm	688
Chapter 52	Havana	710
Chapter 53	Hollywood	731

Downward Spiral ~ In 1919, no one could have been more disheartened to hear Pat was heading to Russia than Agnes MacMillan. Agnes had a ring, a promise and a baby when she said," good-bye" to Pat on May 26. Her gut told her not to reveal the birth of Carol to Pat. We believe she never told him. Indeed, her grandchildren also believe this but no one knows for certain.

If she told him, would he stay and marry her only because of the child? If she told him and he left anyway would that not tell her even more about his commitment to her and the child? Either way, Carol knew Pat would not be at peace until he reconciled his past. For Pat that meant one more chance to fight. Russia was the only active theater available.

There was another reason not to tell Pat about Carol. Agnes knew that she could give Carol a loving father and mother in George and Vesta Hughes. They had not only agreed to raise the child but allow Agnes to be part of Carol's life. Though they actually never adopted Carol, they raised her and allowed "Aunt Agnes" to visit on holidays and birthdays. Indeed, her grandchildren, still living today, knew Agnes as "Aunt Agnes" and referred to the Hughes as "grandma and grandpa."

Unfortunately, Agnes had her eyes set on the future while Pat was trying to rectify his past. Pat's only option was to "finish" his war in Russia and he did. Agnes' was equally committed to providing her daughter with a solid future and she did. The War had altered the personal history of Pat and Agnes, as it had so many others.

continued from page 117

And so, did Pat return from the desert with a clear mind and a resolve to turn a page in his young live? Perhaps. He makes one final attempt to see Agnes but she avoids his calls. Likely, they eventually spoke by phone when he returned from Russia but we can only speculate. We are quite confident that he never saw her again because of his known timeline once he arrived back on U.S. soil.

One thing is certain. He was unnerved by the loss of Agnes. Being a rich man (realize he traveled Russia and China for five months in high form), he began to invest his money. He found himself among some well-to-do circles as a result of his fame and fortune and he enjoyed it. They also enjoyed him.

He invested in the Allen Car business based on his love for the car which brought him through the Gobi Dessert. The business failed. He invested in the Morocco, Indiana farm, likely out of nostalgia for his farming father, then gave it to his brother. He invested in his film "Shadows of the West," out of his genuine concern for the rising Japanize threat, only to see the government shut the film down as too controversial. He agreed to help his friend John McGraw promote Havana and then got caught up in the seedy underworld of Arnold Rothstein. He bought a huge home in Los Angeles and then allowed his wife Virginia and conniving Sarah Otis and her daughter Gwendolyn to live there and host parties well into the early morning on a regular basis. In the end, all these ventures failed and certainly must have taken a great toll on Pat, both financially and emotionally. Was he naive, careless or unlucky? This hardly describes Pat prior to 1920.

But the overriding enigma about Pat's life is, and always has been, centered on his death. Was he murdered or did he take his own life? Was he struck down by the evil around him or choose to give up. Unfortunately, the facts that have come forward in our research, over the past eight years, provide no clear-cut answer. Should it ever be resolved it will not quiet the intrigue of Pat O'Brien. His life either validates or repudiates the American Dream - the belief that one determined man can succeed against all odds. In the end, Pat's life is a testament to hope and a lesson to all who seek the American Dream., today.

Troops Return ~ Hundreds of troops return to Minneapolis, above. Pat arrived in Minneapolis on October 29, 1919 from Seattle following his five month trip through Siberia, Mongolia and China. The next day he was in Chicago where he witnessed dramatic changes in American life. Two weeks later, 684 vets meet in Minneapolis to form the American Legion. Little did Pat know that this new organization of veterans would ask him to star in one of their first projects, the filming of "Shadows of the West," an anti-Japanize silent film starring Lt. Pat O'Brien. The film warned of the rising threat of the Japanize, twenty-two years before "the war to end all wars" resumed in the form of World War II. Pat witnessed the aggressive nature of the Japanize in Vladivostok. It was clear to World War I vets who served in Asia that Japan had serious plans to expand its domain. On December 7, 1941, it was clear to the whole world.

Post-war churn ~ By 1919, the country looked much more like modern day America than in the years prior to World War I. Like in all post-war periods, victorious vets returned and churned their country, as young vets always do. Many an eighteen year-old who goes to war and "sees the world" comes home at twenty-two emboldened. Every war in history has spawned this same phenomenon. But in 1919, Pat spent five months in Russia and Asia. He didn't witness the change in American that was occurring until he arrived in Chicago in October. By then, the transition to the "Roaring 20's" has begun. Just as he leapt into the Momence Quarry on a bet when he was a boy, he jumped into 1920 with abandonment. What he found was a post-victorious country with all the urban excitement and folly of the 20th century known by all, today.

Riots were occurring as vets demanded their old jobs back in northern cities like Chicago, Cleveland and Detroit. Many African-Americans had moved north during the war to fill those jobs. The war-levy had converted to an income tax but was not sufficient, prompting lawmakers in Washington to adopt a wide range of excise taxes. American companies began churning out cars, tennis rackets, firearms, cameras, hunting knives, chewing gum, candy, and cosmetics. America was becoming a modern, urbanized and far less innocent country. It was the true beginning of 20th Century America, an industrial giant rapidly transitioning away from its frontier past.

When Pat's train arrives in Chicago from Seattle after his Russia trip, the new America hits him square. He is about to turn a mere twenty-nine years old. He has just returned from a trip few Americans ever experience. He is rich and known throughout the country. But since his failed meeting with Agnes, he is now alone, returning to his hometown. When a young man, though he may be famous and successful at a young age, returns home at twenty-nine with no prospects in front of him, he feels restless. For Pat, 1920 will be his restless year. He has lost Agnes and knows nothing of Carol, so he makes the only move he can. He heads for New York City where America goes for yet another chance. His book tours and Chautauqua Days are over. That was old America. Hollywood, Havana and the world of business await him. But there are pitfalls in his path - not of the physical kind which Pat could always overcome, but the human kind that are more sinister, harder to anticipate and ultimately more dangerous.

Unknown to Pat is the high interest Arnold Rothstein, John J. McGraw, Charles Stoneham, Sarah Ottis, Virginia Dale and Paul Hurst have in his future. The events of 1920 eventually destroy Pat, leaving mystery in its wake.

TOURISTS FLOCK TO HAVANA FOR WINTER RACING
Chicago Daily Tribune (1872-1963); Jan 18, 1920; ProQuest Historical Newspapers Chicago Tribune (1849 - 1985)
pg. A2

TOURISTS FLOCK TO HAVANA FOR WINTER RACING

Liquor, Open Town, Add to City's Attraction.

HAVANA, Jan. 13.—[Correspondence.]—The social colony from Chicago and other northern points is due to arrive beginning Jan. 20. They are coming down to tropical weather, abundant beverages, and a wide open resort.

William K. Vanderbilt Jr. led the so city pioneers into port, coming as captain of his good yacht the Genesee. He was closely pursued by Mrs. Katharine Dahlgren Pierce and Rena La Montaigne. But the reservations indicate a heavy influx within the week.

Vice President McGraw of the Cuba American Jockey and Auto club—some Cub fans used to call him "Muggsy" in the days of Frank Chance—is to open the new clubhouse adjoining the grand stand at Oriental park Monday. And then you may dally with other matters that may prove just as entertaining and profitable as the horses O, yes, there may be a small game or there nightly if you are a club member

Nice Little Places Galore.

Right now you may be introduced most any night to a branch of Bradley's or to Carter's or other nice little places. Because the Cubans want you to enjoy yourself. True, some book makers got the cold shoulder and drifted out this week on the homeward trail via New Orleans. But, who should worry while the sun shines.

Hotel rooms are scarce, the prices high, and the food Cuban. McGraw asks all his friends to try the restaurant at Oriental park, "Not," as Jawn says, "because I have anything to do with its management, but because I use good Chicago meat and have a chef who knows how to cook a good meal in the American style. And besides, I eat there every day myself."

President C. A. Stoneham and Manager J. J. McGraw of the New York Giants bought a controlling interest in the Havana race track last fall. Martin Nathanson of this city, formerly secretary at Harlem, is racing secretary.

How Pat got involved with the N.Y. Mob

Pat was well known and, through his manager Lee Keedick, met many famous people. John McGraw, manager of the New York Giants baseball team, became a friend of Pat's and invited him to go to Havana for the opening of McGraw's new casino. McGraw was a partner with Arnold Rothstein, famous Jewish mob boss, who fronted the money for the 1919 Chicago White Sox who threw the World Series.

Illinois People on Scene.

The E. A. Cudahy Jrs., pioneers of the expected invasion from Chicago, are here for a few days. Charles B. Brown Jr. of Lake Forest came in today. Lieut. Pat O'Brien of war fame and Illinois birth, is a favorite around the Hotel Plaza.

They have some dances here would _____ _____ _____. For instance, the Rumba, the Congo Wiggle, and the Nanigo. Don't ask your unsophisticated correspondent to describe them. Besides, THE TRIBUNE is a family newspaper.

Drinks! Of course we know you have been waiting for that. Just have a vision. You are sitting under an awning at a sidewalk table in the Malecon, attired in your lightest fabric, and little of that. You are at the Mirimar, reopened for the first time since the war, and famed throughout all Latin America. A tropical moon beaming upon the placid day, silhouettes Morro castle before you. Cuba's far famed military band is playing one hundred yards away. And the most beautiful women of North and South and Central America are promenading.

John J. McGraw was a Hall of Fame baseball player and the long-time manager of the New York Giants baseball team. He took full advantage of baseball's initial use of one umpire by tripping, blocking and impeding a base runner in any way he could while the umpire was distracted by the flight of the ball. McGraw is widely held to be "the best player to become a great manager" in the history of baseball

McGraw's fiery personality made him fascinating to contemporaries outside sports. Gamblers, show-business people, and politicians were drawn to him. As his celebrity grew, McGraw became increasingly involved in various, sometimes questionable, off-field activities. For a while McGraw owned a poolroom in Manhattan with gambler Arnold Rothstein, who later became the principal financial backer of the 1919 World Series fix. McGraw regularly spent winters in Cuba where he and Giants owner Charles Stoneham owned a share of a racetrack and casino. When Stoneham bought the Giants in 1919, McGraw became vice-president of the club and minority owner.

Pat met John McGraw during one of his many visits to New York. In 1920, McGraw and Stoneham opened the grandest hotel, casino and racetrack in Havana, Cuba. Havana was very much the "Vegas" of the post-war era and Stoneham's strategy was to bring famous people to the hotel to draw business. Though Pat resisted at first, McGraw talked him into spending a few weeks in Havana at the beginning of 1920. Having just been rejected by Agnes following his trip to Siberia, Pat stopped at Momence then rushed to New York to meet with his long-time manager Lee Keedick.

By this time, Keedick had been approached by Sarah Ottis, the woman from Springfield, Illinois who had followed Pat's speaking career since 1918. She was the ex-wife of Lt. Colonel Daniel Mortimer Ottis, a noted surgeon on General Pershing's staff. Sarah used Daniel's name to stay active in the military and social circles of Washington. Ottis met a reporter named Virginia Allen at one of Pat's speeches in Washington. Soon they had interest in Pat but for different reasons.

Ottis wanted Pat to consider a role in a new silent film sponsored by the newly formed American Legion and so she began contacting Keedick. Virginia hoped Pat could help her finally land a role in the movies, something she'd sought for nearly a year. Virginia met Pat through her brother Hugh Livingston, a Naval Pilot active after the war. Once Pat agreed to meet film producers from Hollywood, Sarah Ottis convinced Keedick to hold the meeting in Havana at McGraw's hotel. Sarah made certain that she and Virginia were also in attendance. Pat began dating Virginia three weeks prior to the Havana meeting. John J McGraw signed Pat's passport application in Miami as a witness on December 14, 1919, and then the two departed for Havana. McGraw, Keedick, Pat's old friend and now famous Hollywood photographer Ed Hesser, Ottis, Virginia and the entourage of film people spent three weeks in Havana. On January 1, 1920 Pat married Virginia Allen on the veranda of the Plaza Hotel, in Havana, Cuba.

McGRAW NOT TO RETIRE.

Denies That He Would Quit Baseball—Leaves Today for Cuba.

Manager John McGraw of the Giants and Charles A. Stoneham, President of the club, will leave for Havana today, where they will attend the opening of the race track in the Cuban capital. They recently purchased the racing establishment, which will open its Winter season on Thanksgiving Day.

Manager McGraw last night put at rest all rumors to the effect that he expected to retire from the active management of the club next season. "I do not intend to give up baseball," said Manager McGraw. "I will be right out there on the field with the Giants next season as usual."

It had been rumored for some time that McGraw expected to give up his position as field general and pass the responsibility over to Larry Doyle or Christy Mathewson. McGraw expects to be in Cuba only a short time, for both he and President Stoneham expect to be back here in time for the annual meeting of the National League on Dec. 9. After the baseball meetings McGraw will go back to Cuba, but he will return before the end of February, when he expects to take the Giants South on their annual Spring training jaunt.

The New York Times
Published: November 19, 1919
Copyright © The New York Times

John McGraw brought Pat to Havana, Cuba. Pat married VirginiaAllen in Havana on Jan. 1, 1920.

Pat indicates he left his last passport at home in Momence. He also indicates he obtained in in Peking, China.

14th day of December 1919

as soon as possible

Pat's last minute passport application to Cuba, signed by John J. McGraw, manager of the New York Yankees Baseball Team. Pat left his orginial passport at home and had to apply for a new one, December 19, 1919.

DESCRIPTION OF APPLICANT.

Age: 29 years.
Stature: 6 feet, 1 inches, Eng.
Forehead: Medium
Eyes: Grey
Nose: Regular

Mouth: Regular
Chin: Square
Hair: Brown
Complexion: Medium
Face: Long

Distinguishing marks _____

IDENTIFICATION.

Key West, Fla., December 14th, 1919, 19___

I, John J. McGraw, solemnly swear that I am a {native / ~~naturalized~~} citizen of the United States; that I reside at New York, N. Y. that I have known the above-named Pat O'Brien personally for 7 years and know {him / ~~her~~} to be a native citizen of the United States; and that the facts stated in {his / ~~her~~} affidavit are true to the best of my knowledge and belief.

John J. McGraw
Baseball Manager
(Occupation)
New York City
(Address of witness)

→ *Signature of John J. McGuire on Pat's passport December 14, 1919*

his 14th day _____ 19 19

_____
of the U.S. Dist. Court at Key West, Fla.

Applicant desires passport to be sent to the following address:

Cf. American Consul,
Havana, Cuba.

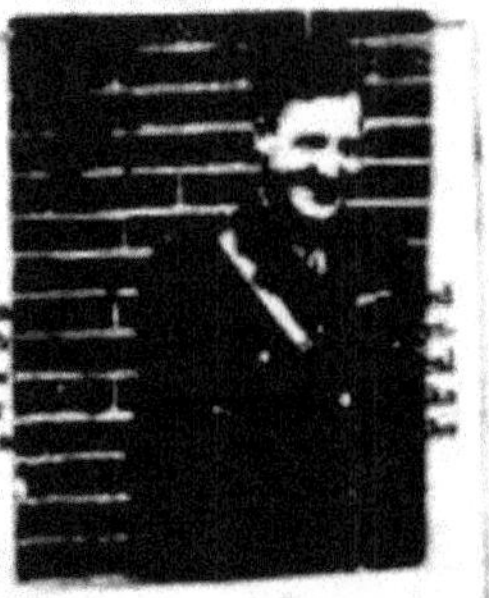

Stoneham & McGraw's holdings

Above: The Oriental Race Track in Havana owned by Charles Stoneham and John J. McGraw.

Below: The Hotel Plaza in Havana where Pat O'Brien and Virginia Allen were married on January 1, 1920.

"Lt. Pat O'Brien"
Timeline
1919 - October 15 - December 19

October 15	Chicago White Sox owner Charles Comiskey denies players involved in alleged throwing of World Series
October 26	Pat arrives in Seattle back from Russia
October 27	Unable to reach Agnes Pat decides to head back home. Arrives in Minneapolis then Chicago Oct 29.
October 30	Pat speaks to Agnes by phone from Momence. Their relationship ends.
November 10	Founding meeting of the American Legion in Minneapolis
November 16	Pat meets with John McGraw, Manager of New York Giants baseball team about Cuba promotion
November 17	Virginia Dale meets Sarah Otis for the first time in Washington, D.C.
December 3	Pat and Hesser meet film-maker Paul Hurst in New York
December 8	Pat meets Virginia Dale at speech in Washington
December 19	King of England announces Pat to be awarded the Military Cross

"Lt. Pat O'Brien" Timeline

1920 - January 1 - December 13

January 1	Pat marries Virginia Dale in Havana, Cuba after a three week courtship
January 18	Pat back in Momence for visit
February 25	Pat moves in Los Angeles
May 15	Pat and Virginia visit Momence
May 23	Pat and Virginia visit his sister in Lowell
June 4	Pat and Virginia head back to California
June 7	Shooting begins for "Shadows of the West"
June 30	Pat invests in Hedding-O'Brien Allen Motor Car dealership in Los Angeles
July	Film shooting continues
August	"Shadows of the West" is released. Federal government orders film shut down to avoid inflaming Japanize Government
October 4	Sarah Ottis and her daughter Guendolen move in with the O'Briens
December 6	At Pat's requests, Clara goes to California to help Pat deal with Sarah Ottis and building chaos
December 13	Pat turns 30 years old

CUPID HIS GOOD ANGEL

LIEUT. PAT O'BRIEN, FORMER R. A. F. FLIER, WINS ANOTHER VICTORY.

Pretty Washington Girl Surrendered to Daring Air Fighter After Heavy Bombardment of Candy and Flowers.

The good angel which has been sitting in the observer's cockpit of Lieut. Pat O'Brien's old lifebus ever since that black haired Irishman first swung his long legs into the pilot's seat of an airplane some half a decade ago hasn't deserted him in the months that have followed his discharge from the R. A. F. of England, although it must be admitted that in recent months the angel has displayed a remarkable resemblance to the winged little, bare little god o' love.

The metamorphosis occurred in this manner. Lieutenant Pat, seeking relief, it may be, from a long dry winter, hopped over to Cuba one day several months ago. The angel then was the same angel that had attended him over the German lines. It grinned at him, as it had grinned when the plane was bouncing about like a cork on the sea midst bursting shrapnel. It seemed to say, "All right, old boy, go as far as you like. I'm with you."

THE ANGEL CHANGES FORM.

But it wasn't prepared for the barrage from a pair of gray eyes into which Lieutenant Pat recklessly plunged on the veranda of a Havana hotel. There was a shiver, a jolt, and the heart of Lieutenant Pat zoomed toward the heavens which are said to be especially kind to lovers and flying men. When the plane of his emotions was righted again, the guardian angel which had been his constant companion for five years was nowhere to be seen. Instead there was the top of a roguish head and the tip of a cupid's bow peaking up over the windshield.

MRS. PAT O'BRIEN, WHO BECAME BRIDE OF R. A. F. PILOT AFTER ROMANTIC COURTSHIP IN CUBA.

The daring Pat didn't take time to identify his new passenger, but loaded up his racks and started out on a combined reconnaisance and bombing expedition. His object was the heart of petite, golden haired Virginia Elizabeth Allen of Washington. There was a Cuban officer hovering in the sun of her smile, but him the dashing R. A. F. fighter drove down out of control with a single burst from his magazine of wit. He then began to release his bombs upon the enemy. Bouquets and candy fell in a constant stream upon her until finally she capitulated. Another had been added to Lieutenant Pat's string of victories.

Kansas City Star
May 5, 1920

Virginia Livingston was divorced when she met Pat. Her name was Virginia Allen but she also used a stage name of Virginia Dale Some records misprinted her name as Virginia Vale another actress not born until 1920. Hollywood records confuse Pat with actor Pat O'Brien who began acting in 1930.

Virginia Livingston Allen O'Brien
Stage Name Virginia Dale - 1920

Who was Sarah Ottis? ~ People knew little of Sarah Ottis until Pat died. The day after his death, Sarah was the only one speaking to the press on behalf of the "bereaved" Virginia. It must have been clear to the press that Mrs. Ottis had developed a confidential relationship with Virginia Allen O'Brien despite the fact that she was not related to Virginia *or* Pat. Sarah and her adult daughter Gwendolyn had actually been living with the O'Brien's since they moved to 2314 N. Commonwealth in Los Angeles in the Spring of 1920

As details surrounding Pat's death came forward, it also became clear that Sarah Ottis had been following Pat O'Brien longer than anyone knew. Ottis told the press she'd "known Lieut. O'Brien for three years. I met him in Chicago," she said, "while working with Gen. Pershing's sister-in-law, Mrs. Jessie Pershing, at a war booth. I became very friendly with him and never had a quarrel with him." If Sarah had her dates right it would indicate she met Pat while he was with the Signal Corps in San Diego and with the Canadians before heading to Europe. That hardly seems likely but it is possible since Daniel and Sarah Ottis were from Springfield, Illinois. This was well before Pat's fame and Sarah would have had no reason or logical opportunity to know Pat in 1917. The impression one gets from her comment is that she was an old friend of Pat. This countered the alleged "suicide note" found in the room where Pat died that described her as "that awful woman."

Virginia was equally confused. She told the press she married Pat in Chicago when, in fact, they were married in Havana. She also stated that Pat was "unbalanced mentally" and that his act was due to that condition. If one believes that Pat did not kill himself then one must hold that his "suicide note" was fabricated. If it was, then none other than Virginia Allen O'Brien or Sarah Ottis would have written it. But if Virginia loved Pat, she would not have written a word. If one believes she did not love Pat but married him for opportunity only, then she could have collaborated with Sarah. Both women were equally capable of such an act in our opinion.

But what of the line in "Pat's letter" that accuses Sarah of breaking up his marriage? If Sarah wrote the letter would this not be an act of self-incrimination? Hardly. It would serve as the perfect deflection away from Ottis and place the action squarely in the deranged mind of Pat O'Brien.

It was not the only time Sarah Ottis would meddle in other's affairs. Her daughter's marriage to Byron Campbell Munson was annulled in 1921 when a Chicago judge agreed with Munson's mother and brother that Mrs. Ottis had played a role in the

Lt. Colonel Daniel Mortimer Ottis

Sarah Ottis was the wife of Daniel Mortimer Ottis, a Springfield, Illinois physician. The couple was originally from Upper Michigan but moved to Springfield where Doctor Ottis began his practice. Ottis was trained at Rush Medical College in Chicago.

As America drew closer to war, Ottis organized a medical unit of doctors, nurses and orderlies under the American Red Cross but it was eventually federalized for service in the United States Army on April, 1917. Unit W was headed by Ottis and served under John J. Pershing in England There were twelve doctors, twenty-one registered nurses, and fifty orderlies, all from Illinois.

The medical unit was drilled at the State Arsenal in Springfield for two months and orderlies received some training as doctors' helpers at St. John's Hospital in Springfield. On January 22, 1918, they were called to Ft. McPherson, Ga., where they trained for military service.

Prior to their departure, Sarah Ottis divorced her husband. She began an active life in women's organizations volunteering around the country. She spent a good amount of time traveling to hear Pat O'Brien speak, hearing his first public speech outside Kankakee Country at Orchestra Hall in Chicago on February 1st.

Ottis and his team sailed overseas May 11, 1918, on the Ascania, landing in England. They were stationed for short intervals in Liverpool, London, Southampton, and Plymouth. At Plymouth he opened a Camp Hospital. The unit was then transferred to Liverpool and assigned to Camp Hospital No. 40, at Camp Knotty Ash, near Liverpool, where they were stationed from June 4, 1918, to May 1, 1919. While at Camp Knotty Ash they were engaged in the hardest of work caused by the flu epidemic. At this place they lost three of their members, Dr. Frank D. Fletcher, James Rollman, and Miss Geneva Casstevens to the disease. In May, 1919, the Unit left for the United States, and were mustered out at Camp Grant, Illinois, May 26, 1919.

Ottis never returned to his wife after the war. Their daughter Gwendolyn lived with him following Pat's death and following her divorce from Byron Munson in 1921. By all accounts, Colonel Ottis was a dedicated physician, a patriot and a selfless leader in the war. While his wife of twenty-one years was a consummate volunteer among the officer's wives and women's organizations at home, she demonstrated motivations different than her husband's.

Daniels Ottis died of a cerebral hemorrhage in 1929 at age 59. The 1940 census showed Sarah Ottis still living in California, making her 66 years old at the time.

How Sarah Ottis stalked Pat O'Brien

About the same time Pat and his brother Buck were boarding the train in Momence, Mrs. Jane Sarah Ottis, wife of Dr. Daniel Mortimer Ottis of Springfield, Illinois was watching the snow covered fields north of Bloomington About the same time Pat and his brother Buck were boarding the train in Momence, Mrs. Jane Sarah Ottis, wife of Dr. Daniel Mortimer Ottis of Springfield, Illinois was watching the snow covered fields north of Bloomington whisk by her train car window on her way to Chicago. Like so many who had read about the exploits of Pat's adventure, she developed a keen interest in his story. She was making the trip to hear Pat speak "for the first time" publically as the Sangamon Journal had reported that week. Sarah Ottis had time on her hands. Her husband had recently gone to war. from **"Lt. Pat O'Brien**, Chapter 36, Page 438

"I heard about your exploits and immediately got on a train to Chicago" she said. "My husband is a medical officer with Pershing's Army. I look forward to hearing you speak again," she said, nodding and holding her hat with both hands in front of her. from **"Lt. Pat O'Brien,"** Chapter 37, Page 443

The woman extended her hand this time which Pat shook and then turned to the next couple waiting in line to meet the famous pilot. Ottis moved along but then stood against the large windows located along the exterior of hall across from Pat observing the reception line all waiting patiently to meet him. "This man really has something," she thought. from **"Lt. Pat O'Brien,"** Chapter 37, Page 444

"Something about a movie," replied Hesser. "Yeah, she said she knew you from Chicago. Apparently, heard you speak or something. She's some big muckety-muck with a group of officer's wives in Washington.

"I remember now," said Hesser. "Her name was Sarah Ottis. Yes, that's right Ottis."

Suddenly, Pat pictured exactly who she was. The lobby at Orchestra Hall in Chicago flashed through his mind and that night in Decatur when she'd commandeered Pat and his brother to meet a bunch of people from Springfield.

> **Grand** — TODAY AND TOMORROW
> Truthful-startling-thrilling
>
> **"SHADOWS OF THE WEST"**
>
> With HEDDA NOVA and the American Ace
> LIEUT. PAT O'BRIEN
>
> A powerful drama of the west.
> Story based upon the Asiatic Question in California.

> **LYRIC**
> LAST TIMES TODAY
> **Shadows of the West**
> A gripping western drama
> Starring
> **Hedda Nova**
> Replete with thrilling climaxes
> —also—
> **Johnny Hines**
> in
> "Torchy's Promotion"
> TOMORROW
> **Harry Carey**
> in
> "THE FOX"

The title of the film was "Shadows of the West." Pat played Jim Kern, the lead. Hedda Nova was Mary with Virginia playing a character named Lucy Norton. Zeliff played Frank Akuri and Ben Corbette played Jim's pal. The plot was a basic one, hero off to the war, leaves girl behind who is accosted while alone and nearly meets her fate until, low and behold, the hero returns in the nick of time. It was a plot as old as storytelling itself. from **"Lt. Pat O'Brien,"** Chapter 53, Page 743

Hedda Nova was born in Odessa, Russia and was also the wife of "Shadows of the West" Director Paul Hurst. Nova was a silent film star but did not act once sound was added to films. This was likely due to her Russian accent.

Popular writing, movies, and the Hearst newspapers in particular, promoted fear of the Japanize following World War I. The film "Patria," produced by Hearst's International Film Service Corp. in 1917, and **"Shadows of the West**," circulated by the American Legion, both portrayed Japanese immigrants as sneaky, treacherous agents of a militaristic Japan seeking to control the West Coast.

McSWAIN THEATRE

The Playhouse of Character

Showing Today

"SHADOWS OF THE WEST"

featuring

Hedda Nova and Lieut. Pat O'Brien

A powerful drama of the west.

Pulsating with thrills, suspense and action. Story based upon the Asiatic question in California.

A burning topic — a coming issue. If you are for America First, you should see this marvelous photoplay.

Showing Today Only!!

Watch for "Nobody's Fool"

Christmas Special 'The Three Musketeers' Monday, December 26th

---

COLONIAL
TODAY AT 2.15, 6.45, 8.30

Is there Anything a Real Western Cowboy Can't Ride? You'll Say Not After Seeing

"Shadows Of The West"

A WESTERN DRAMA WITH HEDDA NOVA AND LIEUT. PAT O'BRIEN

ALSO

HOLMAN DAY PICTURE
NEWS TOPICS—COMEDY

THURSDAY—

Bert Lytell in "The Right that Failed"

BE SURE TO TAKE IN THE

ROYAL

Vaudeville and Picture Combination Show

KAY LAUREL in "LONELY HEART," in six acts

HEDDA NOVA in "SHADOWS OF THE WEST" Six Acts

News ——————— Comedy

Hedda Nova - Pat's female Co-star in "Shadows of the West." Wife of Director Paul Hurst

"Reproduced courtesy of David S. Shields, Broadway Photographs Collection

FEAR OF JAPAN - The motivation for "Shadows of the West."

Japan's victory over China in the Sino-Japanese War in 1895, followed by their defeat of the Russians in the Russo-Japanese War of 1904-05, proved that Japan clearly had interest in territorial expansion. The Japanese Military had shunned the ancient Chinese Samurai military model in favor of the new modern American industrial military, developed during the McKinley-Roosevelt-Taft presidential eras, and it was working.

In World War I, just as in World War II, the Germans found themselves pressing on two fronts, Western Europe and the Eastern Front of Russia. For the British, French, and other Entente powers, this prevented Germany from pouring all resources into France, likely defeating the British and French in rather short order. Indeed, keeping the Germans busy in the East was a major part of Entente strategy to win the West.

The wildcard was a man named Vladimir Lenin who's only interest was defeating his perceived "real enemy," The Russian Czar. The Bolsheviks seize power from the Russian Provisional Government in November 1917 and Lenin signed a temporary peace treaty with the Germans one month later. But White loyalists supporting the Czar hung on until the Red Army had total control. With the help of Britain, Japan, France, Canada, Poland, Italy, Romania, America, and a band of Czech Legions, the old Russian Army fought back and forth along the Trans-Siberian Railroad until the Red Army pushed everyone out to sea at Vladivostok in 1922. More importantly, it kept the Germans in Russia, until the end of the war. The effort to get Americans and others out of Russia following then end of World War I was the melee Pat chose to enter in 1919.

Pat O'Brien, and others who witnessed the aggressive presence of the Japanize at Vladivostok, were convinced that Japan was the next threat to the West. Vladivostok was the marshaling point for all foreign troops heading west toward the advancing Reds. Thus, machismo parading of Entente troops through Vladivostok became a daily occurrence. The subtext of these parades was a demonstration of perceived post-war strength and the Japanese had more troops in Russia than any other country, over 72,000. The Czechs, an army with not country at the time, had 70,000. America had 9,000, the Canadians 4,200, British a mere 1600 and France a token 760 troops. The Japanese were more interested in exploring potential resources in Russia than holding back the Red Army. They paraded more than they fought and continued to occupy Siberia even after other Allied forces had withdrawn in 1922.

Pat was either asked by the military or simply inserted himself into the Siberian Expedition. We find only enough information in our research to speculate about Pat's motivation but it seems clear he had personal reasons for "returning to war." What cannot be ignored, however, are his experiences with the railroad and his proven ability to go "undercover" behind enemy lines. This matched him well to the Siberian mission which was increasingly becoming an "escape to the East" by 1919.

Pat came home convinced of Japanese intentions. Veterans from the Pacific Theater warned of the growing size and intensity of the Japanize military and their influence was strongly present in the newly-formed American Legion. This concern created interest in a film, produced by the American Legion, to warn Americans of the threat of the Japan.

Rumors circulated in California that Japan would organized the wealth and manpower of China to equip armies capable of creating real "yellow peril" along the U.S. Pacific coast. Fear of possible war with Japan, now a powerful country, exacerbated these anxieties. Much of the anti-Japanese activity in the United State, including the Alien Land Law of 1920 banning acquisition of California land by Asians, particularly the Japanese, provided strong protest from Japan.

During this time, numerous anti-Asian sentiments were expressed by politicians and writers, especially on the West Coast, with headlines like "The 'Yellow Peril'" (Los Angeles Times) and "Conference Endorses Chinese Exclusion" (The New York Times), and the later Japanese Exclusion Act. Popular writing, the movies and the Hearst newspapers in particular, promoted the fear.

The films, "Patria," (1917) produced by Hearst's International Film Service Corporation and Pat's "Shadows of the West," (1920) circulated by the American Legion, both portrayed Japanese immigrants as sneaky, treacherous agents of a militaristic Japan seeking to control the West Coast.

ALIEN LAND LAW of 1920

In California, anti-Asian feelings were the strongest. Asians were buying farmland in California and the possibility of Japanese landowners controlling the agriculture industry in California was perceived as a real threat. The California Alien Land Law of 1920 was passed in reaction to this growing anti-Japanese sentiment. The law upgraded the 1913 Alien Land Law which was doing little to stem Japanese immigration to California.

MOVIE REVIEW of "Shadows of the West," 1920

"Shadows of the West" is a mix of "yellow peril" sensationalism and ordinary Wild West shenanigans. War hero Lt. Pat O'Brien stars as Jim Kern, a cowpoke who enlists in the U.S. Army to fight in "the war to end all wars." Returning from the front, Kern finds that an "Oriental," Frank Akuri (Seymour Zeliff), has not only forced his sweetheart, Mary (Hedda Nova), off her ranch but is planning to colonize the United States on behalf of Japan. Jim, naturally, takes umbrage to this unwholesome scheme and when Akuri kidnaps Mary for wholly prurient reasons, the cowboy and a war buddy (Pat Corbett) put everything they have learned fighting the Evil Hun to good use. Mary is rescued in the nick of time and the American West is liberated from tyranny once and for all. The film opened in a mysterious room fitted with wireless apparatus by which a Japanese man picked out prices controlling the state-wide vegetable market. Spies darted in and out of the scenes, Japanese were shown dumping vegetables into the harbor to maintain high prices; two white girls were abducted by a group of Japanese men only to be rescued, at the last moment, by Jim Kern (Lt. Pat O'Brien) and a squad of American Legionnaires.

THE AMERICAN LEGION - Their role in "Shadows of the West"

The American Legion provided financial investment for "Shadows of the West" and exhibited it around the country. Pat also invested in the film. The American Legion sought to increase awareness of the potential for Japanese influence and power in the world following World War I.

CENSORED - Virginia Dale eliminated from 2nd version.

"Shadows of the West" was produced in eight reels in 1920 but the U.S. Government thought it to be too controversial due to its inflammatory characterization of Japan. Motion Picture Producing Co. of America reduced the film to five reels, eliminating the worst of the "yellow peril" propaganda in favor of the more wholesome Western aspects. As such, it was finally redistributed by National Exchanges in 1921 after Pat's death. Our research found showings as late as 1922 in theaters across the country. Virginia Dale, Pat's wife, was said to be furious that her parts in the film were eliminated during the editing process, thus adding addition fuel to the concept that she may have been motivated to eliminate her husband with the help of Sarah Ottis.

EDWIN B. HESSER - Pat's link to Hollywood

Ed Hesser was a close friend of Pat's for the last ten years of Pat's life. Pat was twenty when they met and Hesser was saw Pat in the last week of Pat's life. Hesser lived till 1962 and is considered, along with George Hurrell, to have virtually invented celebrity portraiture as we know it today.

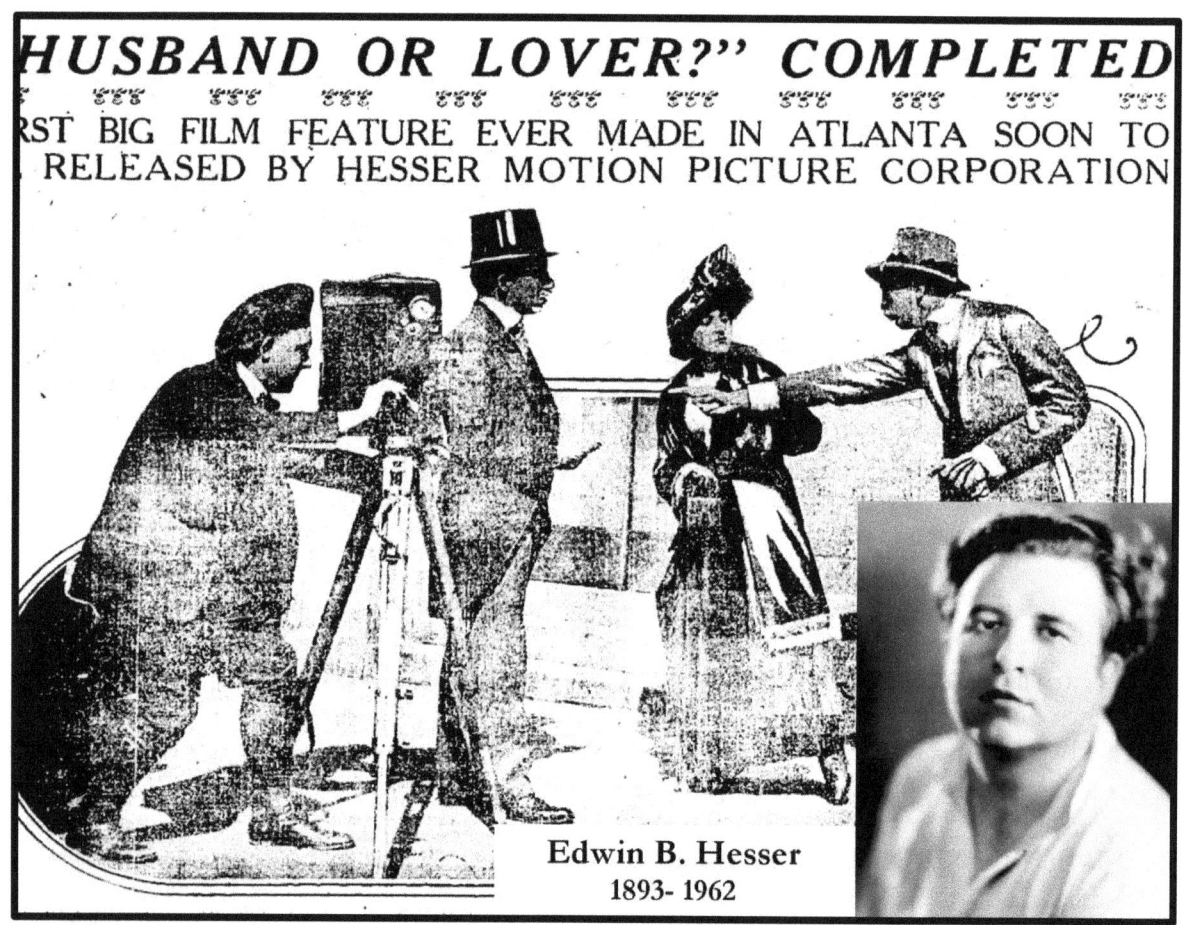

Edwin B. Hesser
1893- 1962

EDWIN B. HESSER ~ The huge impact of Ed Hesser in the life of Pat O'Brien cannot be overstated. "Hess," as Pat often called him, was likely one of the most famous people Pat knew. Hesser was highly connected to powerful and influential people in the New York entertainment industry and the entire film industry of Hollywood. There is little doubt that Hesser connected Pat to many rich and famous people on both coasts and surely played a role in putting Pat in the silent film, "Shadows of the West." Pat and Hesser were friends as far back as 1910 when the two aviation enthusiasts first built and tested their own crude airplanes in California.

Born into a theatrical family with a theatrical company manager as a father and an art teacher as a mother, Hesser became involved in theatre, drawing, sculpture, painting, and commercial photography at the age of 17. In 1918, Hesser was commissioned as Captain in the Photographic Section of the U.S. Army Signal Corps where he reorganized the motion picture photographic division of the Army. During that time, he presented pat to a number of audiences during Pat's speaking tours. Later that year, Hesser received an honorable discharge and moved to New York City. Hesser was employed as a writer and producer by First National Pictures, and then started his own independent photographic studio.

Hesser moved to Los Angeles in 1920 to continue to work for First National Pictures, where he became the portrait photographer for the studio's stars. Today, his photography is considered art and demands high prices among the photographic art community. Among Edwin Hesser's photography clients are Carole Lombard, Joan Crawford, Jean Harlow, Mary Pickford, Myrna Loy, and Douglas Fairbanks, Sr.

OTHER EVENTS OF 1920

Pat and Virgina sell farm to Elmer

This Indenture Witnesseth, That the Grantors Pat Alva O'Brien and Elizabeth V. O'Brien his wife of the Town of Momence in the County of Kankakee and State of Illinois, for and in consideration of the sum of Thirty Thousand Dollars, in hand paid.Conveys and warrants to Elmer E. O'Brien of the County of Newton and State of Indiana, the following described real estate to-wit:

The South half of Section Twenty Nine (29) township Thirty (30) N. Range Nine (9) west of Second Principal Meridian, except the South west quarter of the South West quarter of said Section. All situated in Newton County State of Indiana.

Grantee assumes and agrees to pay three certain Mortgages or Trust Deed in amount of $17100 and interest thereon, also all taxes and special assessments., hereby releasing and waiving all rights under and by virtue of the Homestead exemption Laws of this St te, Indiana.

In Witness whereof the said Pat Alva, 'Brien and Elizabeth V. O'Brien, his wife have hereunto set their hands and seals.

Dated thes 25 day of May A.D. 1920.

(Revenue Stamps $13.00) Pat Alva O'Brien.....(Seal)
Elizabeth V. O'Brien..Seal

State of Illinois, Kankakee County, SS:

Before me Victor T. Brassard a Notary Public in and for said County and State Personally appeared Pat A.va O'Brien and Elizabeth V. O'Brien, his wife and acknowledged the execution of the annexed deed to be their voluntary act and deed.
Witness my hand and Notarial Seal this 25th. day of May 1920.

(Notarial Seal) Victor T. Brassand
My Com. Exp Feb. 11" 1924. Notary Public.

I certify that the Deed of which the above is a true copy was recorded June 8" 1920 at 3 o'clock P.M.

Edgar Steward
Recorder Newton County.

O'Brien Home Torn Down

The old O'Brien property now owned by Mr and Mrs. John Lundstrum, corner River and Market streets has been sold for lumber to be used elsewhere and is being torn down this week. This removes one of the oldest landmarks in the city.

PAT O'BRIEN IS ON AUTO ROW.

Hedding-O'Brien Motor Co. to Handle the Allen.

Famous Aviator Has Wild List of Experiences.

Tests Out Machine Under Most Trying Circumstances.

Automobile Row has now one of the heroes of the World War and globe trotter as the local representative for the Allen car. Mr. O'Brien has made connections with S. A. Hedding. This new firm will be known as the Hedding-O'Brien Motor Company. They will be temporarily located at 612 West Twelfth street.

SOME EXPERIENCE.

Lieut. O'Brien is the officer of the Royal Flying Corps who fell 8000 feet, after being shot and rendered unconscious, and upon landing was captured by the Germans. After being held prisoner for a short while, Lieut O'Brien escaped, and made his way through Germany by traveling nights and hiding out through seventy-one days of terrific strife.

Mr. O'Brien has fought under eight flags and six wars, and has a record that has only been duplicated by a few men in this world. Mr. O'Brien became acquainted with the Allen car while crossing the Gobi Desert in Mongolia in 1918, traveling 700 miles across the Uda Desert from Calgan, China, to Urga, Mongolia, and the splendid way that this car stood up under the 700 miles of gruelling work, absolutely sold Mr. O'Brien on the merits of the Allen.

AN OLD-TIMER.

His associate, S. A. Hedding, formerly of Minneapolis, Minn., has been in the automobile business for the past ten years. Mr Hedding has been sales manager for several large distributors in Minneapolis, and will be of great aid to the new firm in handling the Allen car in Los Angeles

It is also their plan to take on another line of cars which are now on the way from the East, but will not be announced until their arrival on the Coast

S.A. Hedding.   Pat O'Brien.

Famous Aviator in Auto Game.

Lieut. Pat O'Brien, who, with Mr. S. A. Hedding, has taken over the distribution for the Allen motor car in Los Angeles territory. The Hedding-O'Brien Company expects to start a vigorous sales and service campaign in the near future. Lieut. Pat O'Brien has had enough wild and thrilling war experiences to qualify him for any sort of a job on automobile row.

> The Hedding-O'Brien Motor Car Company was one of six newly established dealerships created to consolidate inventory from other smaller dealers and sell off inventory. Being the sales manager for several large distributors in Minneapolis, C.A. Hedding was asked by Allen Car to find local investors for the new dealerships. If he found an investor Hedding would have no risk. If cars sold, he'd make money. If they didn't, Hedding's separate agreement with Allen Car assured he would be made whole. Pat would lose his entire investment should cars fail to sell. Hedding would get inventory equal to his investment. By November 1st, it was evident that the dealership was not succeeding. *from* "Lt. Pat O'Brien

Part IX
Final Days

Chapter Reference

PART IX ~ Final Days

Corresponding Chapters in "Lt. Pat O'Brien"

Chapter 54 Alexandria Hotel   749
Chapter 55 Last Train Home   772

Final Days ~ And just like that, Pat O'Brien, a kid full of life and a man bigger than life is dead in a Los Angeles hotel. He is thirty years old. Had he been killed in a car accident or perhaps succumbed over time to an illness, the world, his family, and the people of Momence could have confirmed his greatness for a hundred years, void of the implications that, like us, he was vulnerable.

If he is killed by his own gun, Pat O'Brien emerges from history very much like us. Should it ever be proven that he died from the bullet of a murderer, his life of optimism and triumph is confirmed for all of us. "Finding Pat O'Brien" is about discovering that facts of his life, the truth surrounding his death, the nature of his being and, at long last, the nature of our own lives.

The search for Pat O'Brien began early in the morning on December 18, 1920 and continues today. The central question about Pat's life will forever be linked to his death. Despite our eight-plus years of research we are, sadly, no closer to the truth regarding Pat's death then the world was a millennium ago.

Following a rush of activity by friends, family, admirers and hundreds of speculative press, Pat was quietly laid to rest in the Momence Cemetery in 1920 with no marker. Practically, Maggie and the O'Brien family probably could not afford to buy a stone. In reality, the shame associated with suicide during this time offered little motivation to overtly celebrate his legend. Yet the O'Briens and everyone who knew Pat in Momence believed their favorite son would not have taken his own life. That question was laid aside in 1920 and not debated again until 2007 when a small group of people from Momence, likely the last of a generation to know Pat's story, saw to it that Pat O'Brien's grave was appropriately adorned and his life properly memorialized.

"Lt. Pat O'Brien" Timeline

Final Days 1920

July	Pat and Virginia begin to argue about money.
August 1	Pat and Virginia travel to Detroit to visit Hedding. They stop in San Francisco to visit Pat's old friends.
August 16	Final shooting resumes on "Shadows of the West"
September 27	Japanese-Americans in Los Angeles hold a press conference to announce effort to prevent showing release of "Shadows of the West."
September 28	Sarah Ottis arrives in Los Angeles with daughter Gwendolyn and moves in with Pat and Virginia.
October 4	Pat speaks to Los Angeles Preacher group and local politicians to calm fears surrounding film. Preview of film is shown to these groups on October 8.
October 10	T.F. Booker sues Cinema Craft, Inc. claiming he was defrauded of $100,000 investment in "Shadows" film. Pat tells Virginia he invested $5,000 in the film.
October 15	"Shadows of the West" opens in Los Angeles. Sarah and Virginia hold a huge party at the O'Brien house. Parties continue through October. Pat spends increasing nights at Hamilton Hotel to avoid the melee at home.
November 2	Paul Hurst tells Pat that the government is shutting down "Shadows of the West" due to sensitivity with the Japanese government.

"Lt. Pat O'Brien" Timeline

1920 Final Days

November 24	Pat calls his sister Clara and asked her to come to Los Angeles to "help him out." She agrees.
November 26	Pat and Virginia are served a notice of eviction of their large home. Virginia has failed to make payments.
November 27	Pat visits old friend Virgil Moore. He advises Pat to move from expensive Commonwealth Avenue home.
December 6	Clara arrives in Los Angeles.
December 9	Pat visits his counselor Dr. Seager. Pat comes home and learns of the birthday party planned for him by Sarah and Virginia. He attempts to throw Sarah and her daughter out of the house then lets them return at the advice of Virginia.
December 14	Pat receives a letter indicating he will be given the British Military Cross in a ceremony in San Francisco on December 18
December 16	Pat is in San Francisco to receive his award - visits old friends in Richmond. He decides to go home and fails to appear to receive his award.
December 17	Virginia and Sarah get a room at the Hamilton Hotel following a fight with Pat. Pat learns of their departure from Gwendolyn and heads to the hotel to make amends. Pat places a call to Virgil Moore.
December 18	Pat is found by a hotel orderly at 2:00 a.m. in his hotel room with a bullet through his head.

FIRST REPORTS OUT OF LOS ANGELES

FAMOUS AVIATOR IS FOUND DEAD

LOS ANGELES, Dec. 17.—Lieutenant Pat O'Brien, famous world war aviator, was found dead in a room in a downtown hotel here tonight. The police said there was a bullet wound in the forehead and a revolver nearby.

Lieutenant O'Brien figured in a sensational escape from a German internment camp in 1918 after he had been shot down within the enemy lines. He walked for weeks, travelling at night, until he reached the Belgian border and crossed, almost exhausted, into neutral territory, eventually returning to this country. His home formerly was in Illinois.

Lt. Pat O'Brien, famous war aviator, was found dead in a hotel in Los Angeles this morning with a bullet wound in his forehead and a revolver lying near by.

Suicide

News of Pat's death flashed across the wires instantly. First reports indicated he was found dead in the Hamilton Hotel with no mention of a cause.

But quickly stories reported he committed suicide and suffered mentally. This was based on some very proactive statements from none other than Sarah Ottis who had positioned herself as the family spokesperson. Sarah was quoted more in newspaper reports than anyone else in the first few days.

Doctor Walter Seager, described as Pat's "friend and physician," also made statements about Pat's "equilibrium" brought on by war and some of Pat's failed enterprises.

The police concluded Pat died of his own hand, giving little detail in the papers about the basis for the findings. At the request of family and friends, the police conducted a second investigation but came to the same conclusion.

Virginia was unavailable to the press and stayed hidden in her room 'distraught,' according to Sarah Ottis. About one week later she gave a statement to the press collaborating and elaborating on Sarah's initial statements.

Lt. Pat O'Brien, famous war aviator, was found dead in a hotel in Los Angeles this morning with a bullet wound in his forehead and a revolver lying near by.

O'BRIEN, MOVIE ACTOR, SUICIDES

LOS ANGELES, Dec. 18.—Hundreds of persons, prominent in the local moving picture colony with whom he had been associated, were shocked today to learn that Lieut. Pat O'Brien, officer of the Royal Flying Corps and a war aviator, had killed himself in a fashionable downtown hotel, shortly before last midnight. The act followed an unsuccessful effort to effect a reconciliation with his wife, known as "Virginia Dare", from whom he had been separated. Gen. Howard C. Seager, who had been O'Brien's physician, was quoted today as saying he believed the aviator was mentally unhealthy, due to his war experiences.

HERO A SUICIDE

LIEUTENANT PAT-RICK A. O'BRIEN, whose escape from German prison camp was one of notable adventures of the war.

LIEUT. PAT O'BRIEN FOUND DEAD TODAY

Lieut. Pat O'Brien, Who Lectured Here, Kills Self

"Pat" O'Brien, late lieutenant in the Canadian Royal Flying Corps, committed suicide at his California home on Saturday from despondency over attempts to become reconciled with his wife, a former moving picture actress.

Lieutenant O'Brien appeared at the Chestnut street hall near the close of the war, and recited his adventures to a Harrisburg audience. After a three thousand foot fall behind the German lines and several months in a German hospital, Lieutenant O'Brien escaped by jumping from a hospital train.

Later after wandering for nearly three months and living on anything he could get his hands on, O'Brien dug a hole beneath the charged barbed wire on the Dutch border and escaped to Holland.

He was received by the King of England and decorated. Coming back to America he was on the lecture platform for a number of months, at the same time making exhibition flights.

FAMOUS AIRMAN TAKES HIS LIFE IN HOTEL ROOM

LOS ANGELES, Dec. 19.—Lieut. Pat O'Brien, who obtained a commission in the Royal Air Force in Canada and became a war hero while serving at the front in that branch of the British army, committed suicide by shooting, early today in the Alexandra Hotel.

"With all my war record I am just like the rest of the people—a little bit of clay," he wrote in a note found in his room. "Only a coward would do what I am doing." The note indicated that failure to bring about a reconciliation with his wife who is "Virginia Dare" in motion pictures, led to O'Brien's act.

Lieut. O'Brien, a native of California, enlisted in the Royal Air Force in Canada, and soon gained fame by daring exploits. Once he fell several thousand feet, after a battle with a German flier, and landed behind the enemy lines.

He was put in a German field hospital. Later, when bound for a German prison camp, he jumped from the speeding train and for 72 days wandered through Germany and Luxembourg, finally arriving in Holland, when he made his way into Belgium. Two years ago he fell 2,000 feet at Kelly field, San Antonio, Tex. and escaped with a broken nose.

He related his hardships to King George at Buckingham Palace after his return to Great Britain.

O'BRIEN, FAMOUS ACE, KILLS SELF

Los Angeles, Cal., Dec. 18.—Hundreds of prominent personages in the local moving picture colony with whom he had recently been associated, were shocked today to learn that Lieutenant Pat O'Brien, officer of the Royal Flying Corps and famous as a war aviator, had killed himself in a fashionable hotel, while lately shortly before midnight.

Indications that the had failed to effect his husband reconciled of a former actress than a tragedy had terminated was added and before the O'Brien suicide.

Mrs. O'Brien, living on a cot in her room at the hotel and suffering from the shock, reportedly moved and dramatically shook her this morning in a sensible over her dead husband, that approximate his first identity.

CONFIRM FINDINGS; WAR HERO SUICIDE

LOS ANGELES, Dec. 26.—Captain Charles F. Moffatt, in charge of the detective bureau of the local police department, today announced that a second investigation of the death of Lieutenant Pat O'Brien, war aviator, Dec. 17, confirmed the findings in the first investigation that O'Brien committed suicide.

CE PRESS · REPORTER.

MOMENCE, ILLINOIS, FRIDAY, DECEMBER 24, 1920   NUMBER 52

Momence Paper Christmas Eve 1920

LIEUT. PAT O'BRIEN ENDS HIS LIFE IN WEST

World Famed Aviator Ends His Brilliant Career in a Tragic Manner.

WILL BE BURIED HERE MONDAY

Last Message of Lieutenant Pat O'Brien Addressed to His Wife.

DEAR WIFE:

Only a coward would do what I am doing, but I guess I am one. With all my war record, I am just like the rest of the people in this world—a little bit of clay, and to you, my sweet little wife—I go thinking of you, and my dear, sweet mother, my sisters and brothers.

And may the just God that answered my prayers in the two days that I spent in making my escape from Germany, once more answer them.

And bring trouble, sickness, disgrace and more bad luck than anyone else in this world has ever had, and curse forever that awful woman that has broken up my home and taken you from me; the woman who stood in my home and gave (several words blurred), she caused this life of mind that a few moments ago was happy, to go on that sweet, adventurous death.

Please send what you find to my dear mother in Momence, Illinois.

To the five armies I have been in; the birds, the animals I love so well, to my friends; to all the world of adventure—I say Good-bye.

                          Pat.

No one from the O'Brien family ever believed that Pat comitted suicide. But first reports out of Los Angeles indicated he had. That story raced across the press in the United States. Pat's sister Clara was in L.A. at the time and immediately demanded a second inquriy. The Los Angeles Police obliged, sending the same man who repeated his claim.

Widow of Pat O'Brien Thinks Strain of War Caused Mental Aberration and His Killing

LOS ANGELES, Cal., Dec. 20.—Authorities investigating the tragic death of Lieut. Pat O'Brien, noted war hero, today were confident he had taken his own life in a fit of insanity prompted by his battle experiences. O'Brien recently was under great strain as a result of opposition he encountered while starring in an anti-Japanese photoplay called "Shadows of the West."

It was stated no further probe would be made.

The aviator's widow seconded the police conclusion. She declared she had feared to meet her husband the morning of his death because of a premonition that a tragedy was impending.

Mrs. O'Brien, lying on a cot in her room at a hotel and suffering from the shock, emphatically denied the statement made by her husband in a suicide note that Mrs. Sarah Ottis was responsible for their troubles.

"I was in mortal fear of Pat and was afraid to live with him for fear he would take my life. That is why I dreaded to go to his room when he telephoned that he wanted to talk with me," said Mrs. O'Brien.

"Mrs. Ottis was just a friend to us, more like a mother than anything else, and I do not know what I would have done if she had not comforted me in my terrible distress. She was not to blame and I feel I must contradict this awful statement left by my husband.

"Mr. O'Brien and I were married a year ago. We came to Los Angeles in June and he and I both worked in motion pictures. As time went on he became subject to terrible fits of temper. He often struck me.

"Mrs. Ottis, who had known both of us for several years, came from Chicago two months ago to visit us."

Mrs. Ottis said: "I have known Lieut. O'Brien for three years. I met him in Chicago while working with Gen. Pershing's sister-in-law, Mrs. Jessie Pershing, at a war booth. I became very friendly with him and never had a quarrel with him. I had accompanied Mrs. O'Brien to a hotel at her request. I always advised Mrs. O'Brien to return to her husband if she wanted to."

The $150,000 fortune of Pat O'Brien, romantic popular idol and war hero who committed suicide here, is missing, according to Merwin O'Brien, his brother, who arrived today from Oakland.

The famous ace who took his life when his wife, a movie actress, refused to see him, had the fortune in Liberty Bonds and other securities less than a year ago, his brother said.

"Pat always led a model life and I cannot believe he allowed such a large sum of money to become dissipated," Merwin O'Brien said. "He had $50,000 in cash in banks in New York, Chicago and San Francisco; $50,000 in steel stocks, and $25,000 in Liberty Bonds. His book, 'Outwitting the Hun,' netted him $15,000, and he realized money from magazine articles and lectures."

O'Brien's widow refused to see the brother today when he called at the Alexandria, Merwin O'Brien said.

LIEUT. PAT O'BRIEN COMMITS SUICIDE

Aerial War Hero Shoots Himself Following the Estrangement of His Wife.

FOUND HE WAS 'ONLY CLAY'

"Only a Coward Would Do What I Am Doing," He Wrote— Curses Another Woman.

LOS ANGELES, Dec. 18.—Lieutenant Pat O'Brien, veteran of the British Royal Flying Corps, killed himself in a hotel room here early today shortly after he had talked over the telephone with his wife, from whom he had been estranged. Mrs. O'Brien, through friends, today said she was convinced that her husband was unbalanced mentally and that his act was due to that condition.

Lieutenant O'Brien left a note addressed to his wife in which he spoke of himself as "like the rest of people—a little bit of clay."

In a letter he bade farewell to his wife, mother and sisters, and continued: "And may the just God that answered my prayers in those seventy-two days that I spent in making my escape from Germany once more answer them.

"And bring trouble, sickness, disgrace and more bad luck than any one else in this world has ever had, and curse forever that awful woman * * * that has broken up my home and taken you from me, the woman that stood in my home and gave (several words blurred). She caused this life of mine that just a few moments ago was happy to go on that sweet adventure of death."

Mrs. O'Brien denied that any third person had interfered in the family affairs and said the woman named by O'Brien as responsible had been introduced to her by her husband and had joined her at her request because she did not wish to live unprotected.

Mrs. O'Brien was a bride of a few months. She declined to give her former name or any facts concerning herself and she was secluded under a physician's care. Friends of O'Brien said his wife was formerly a newspaper woman in Washington, where he met her, and that she wrote under the name of Virginia Dale or Virginia Dare. While O'Brien was engaged in motion picture work here last Summer his wife did some studio work, but she was said to be unemployed at present.

"Only a coward would do what I am doing," O'Brien wrote.

Lieutenant O'Brien was suffering from a "wrecked nervous equilibrium," according to Dr. Walter Seager, his friend and physician. Dr. Seager said Lieutenant O'Brien probably had been suffering from the results of his experiences during the war.

The widow was prostrated tonight in a room in the same hotel where her husband killed himself. Through a close friend, Mrs. Sarah Ottis of Springfield, Ill., Mrs. O'Brien expressed the opinion her husband had been mentally unbalanced and that he had planned to kill her had she responded to his telephonic request for her to meet him.

Mrs. Ottis, it developed later, was the woman mentioned in the message O'Brien addressed to his wife as having interfered in their family affairs. She said she could attribute the aviator's statements only to his mental condition. Mrs. O'Brien declared Mrs. Ottis never had interfered between her husband and herself.

"Mrs. Ottis has been more of a mother to me than anything else," said she. "Mrs. Ottis came out here from Chicago two months ago to visit us," Mrs. O'Brien continued. "Last Tuesday, after Mr. O'Brien had given way to a terrible fit of temper, in which he broke my finger, I left our home and engaged a room at a hotel.

"Mrs. Ottis joined me at my request. She had nothing to do with my leaving home. I simply decided I could no longer live with my husband.

"Mr. O'Brien found out where we were and engaged rooms in the same hotel. I believe he intended to kill me as well as himself."

Mrs. Ottis added, "I was staying with Mrs. O'Brien because I was afraid damage would be done by her husband. He has been irrational for several weeks."

O'Brien's sister, Mrs. Clara Clegg, came here recently from Momence, Ill. His brother, Merwin, is expected here soon from San Francisco to assume charge of the body and its removal to Momence for burial.

Lieutenant Pat O'Brien, a native of California, but whose home was at Momence, Ill., when he first took up aviation, was one of the first American flyers to win distinction in the war. Early in the war, before the entrance of the United States, he went to Canada and enlisted in the Royal Flying Corps and soon gained fame for many daring exploits.

In the Summer of 1917 he fell several thousand feet in a battle between six British and twenty German aviators and landed behind the enemy lines. He recovered consciousness in a German hospital. Lieutenant O'Brien was held for several weeks at Courtrai, Belgium, and was started for a prison camp in Germany.

He escaped by jumping from a train going at a rate of thirty miles an hour while sixty miles inside of Germany and wandered for seventy-two days through that country, Luxemburg and Belgium before he reached the neutral country of Holland and reported to the nearest British consul.

Lieutenant O'Brien was acclaimed as a hero both in England and the United States. He was received by King George at Buckingham Palace. Upon his return to the United States he was enthusiastically received and appeared in public as a lecturer and a monologist. After the war he gave exhibition flights at most of the flying fields in the country in connection with his lecture tours.

Two years ago Lieutenant O'Brien fell 2,000 feet at Kelley Field, San Antonio, Texas, and escaped with a broken nose.

New York Times report lacks any commentary regarding cause of death.

Story purports Pat committed suicide but offers only opinions rather than evidence.

Story features statements by Sara Ottis and Virginia

Story states that Virginia "declined to give her former name or any facts concerning herself."

Ottis acts as spokesperson for Virginia who is "secluded under physician's care."

AIR HERO IS A SUICIDE OVER BREAK WITH WIFE

Lieut. Pat O'Brien, Daredevil, Kills Himself in Los Angeles —Says He Is Coward.

N.Y. World — Dec. 19, 1920

LOS ANGELES, Cal., Dec. 18.—Lieut. Pat O'Brien, one of the most daring and spectacular aviators in the British Royal Flying Corps during the war, ended his adventurous life in his room at the Alexandria Hotel here to-day because he had failed to become reconciled with his wife, a motion picture actress.

"With all my war record I am just like the rest of the people—a little bit of clay. Only a coward would do what I am doing," he wrote shortly before he fired the shot that killed him.

After mentioning in endearing terms his wife, his mother and his sisters, the note reads:

"And may the God that answered my prayers when I was making my escape from Germany once more answer them, and bring trouble, sickness, disgrace and more bad luck than any one else in the world has ever had and curse forever that awful woman that has broken our home and has taken you from me.

"She has caused this life of mine, that just a few minutes ago was so happy, to go on that sweet adventure of death."

Lieut. O'Brien had married less than a year ago Miss Virginia Elizabeth Allen of Washington. They came to Los Angeles last June. He was thirty years old.

Through a close friend Mrs. Sarah Ottis of Springfield, Ill., Mrs. O'Brien expressed the opinion her husband had been mentally unbalanced and that he had planned to kill her had she responded to a telephone request to meet him.

Mrs. Ottis, it developed later, was the woman mentioned in the message O'Brien addressed to his wife as having interfered in their family affairs. Mrs. O'Brien declared Mrs. Ottis never had interfered between her husband and herself.

"Mrs. Ottis has been more of a mother to me than anything else," said she. "Last Tuesday, after Mr. O'Brien had given way to a fit of temper, in which he broke my finger, I left our home and engaged a room at a hotel. Mrs. Ottis joined me at my request. She had nothing to do with my leaving home. I simply decided I could no longer live with my husband."

Mrs. O'Brien was a bride of a few months. She declined to give her former name or any facts concerning herself, and she was secluded under a physician's care. Friends of O'Brien [said] his wife was formerly a newspaper woman in Washington, where [he m]et her, and that she wrote under

Lieut. PATRICK ALVA O'BRIEN

the name of "Virginia Dale" or "Virginia Dare." While O'Brien was engaged in motion picture work here last summer his wife did some studio work, but she was said to be unemployed at present.

Lieut. O'Brien, a native Californian, has seen service in five wars. He was a member of an aero squadron in Texas when the war broke out, and early in the conflict enlisted in Canada. His most spectacular of a number of exploits that gained him a wide reputation for his daring was when he fell several thousand feet behind the German lines with a bullet in his throat after a battle with a German flyer.

His unconscious body was found lying near the machine, which he had succeeded in keeping under partial control until the landing, and he was taken to a military hospital. From here, when he was cured of his wound, the flyer was sent by train to a prison camp in the interior.

During the night O'Brien leaped through a window of the moving train into the fields, and for seventy-two days wandered about the country, hiding by day and travelling by night, living on such food as he could steal from the fields, and clad in a tattered civilian garment over his uniform. Finally he reached the Dutch border and reached neutral ground by digging under the electrically charged wire fence with a stick and his bare hands.

When he returned to England he had an audience for nearly an hour with King George at Buckingham Palace. Two years ago O'Brien had another fall at Kelley Field, San Antonio, in which he broke his nose.

LIEUT. PAT O'BRIEN IS A SUICIDE

Commits Deed After Talk Over Phone With Wife

LIEUTENANT PAT O'BRIEN, Aviation hero, who committed suicide in a Los Angeles hotel.

NOTED AVIATOR, SUFFERING FROM EXPERIENCES IN WAR, ENDS LIFE IN LOS ANGELES

LOS ANGELES, Dec. 18.— Lieutenant Pat O'Brien, officer of the Royal Flying Corps during the world war, who, according to a police report, committed suicide by shooting himself at a hotel here last night, was suffering from a "wrecked nervous equilibrium," according to Dr. Walter Seager, his friend and physician.

Dr. Seager said Lieutenant O'Brien probably had been suffering from the results of his experiences during the war.

The widow, who, it was said, formerly was Virginia Allen, a newspaper woman of Washington, D. C., was prostrated tonight in a room in the same hotel where her husband killed himself.

Through a close friend, Mrs. Sarah Otis, of Springfield, Ill., Mrs. O'Brien expressed the opinion her husband had been mentally unbalanced and that he had planned to kill her, had she responded to his telephonic request for her to meet him last night.

Mrs. Otis said Mrs. O'Brien's belief that she narrowly escaped death at her husband's hands was based on the fact that she was not mentioned in a message, unofficially termed a will, that was found; and that none of a series of mementoes the aviator had laid out, labelled on his bed, bore her name.

Although it was understood O'Brien had only one brother, Merwin O'Brien of San Francisco, the document unofficially termed a will was addressed "to Brother Elmer."

It follows:

"Please see that Clara Clegg, my sister, gets $1000 from my farm in Indiana, as I owe it to her. After you take what you have coming to you, see that mother gets all the rest.

(Signed) "PAT O'BRIEN."

His sister, Mrs. Clegg, came here recently from Momence, Ill. His brother Merwin is expected here soon from San Francisco to assume charge of the body and its removal to Momence, for burial.

There will be no inquest, the coroner having announced he was convinced the aviator killed himself.

Lieut. Pat O'Brien Suicides in Los Angeles

(By Associated Press.

Los Angeles, Dec. 18—Lieut. Pat O'Brien, World famous aviator, was found dead in a downtown hotel late tonight. The police said a bullet hole was in his forehead and a revolver found by his side.

It is known that O'Brien had threatened to kill himself owing to estrangement from his wife, to whom he had attempted to bring about reconciliation.

Lieut. O'Brien, an American whose home was at Momence, Ill., went to Canada early in the war and entered the British air service.

He was captured by the Germans but escaped by leaping from a fast moving train. He made his way thru enemy teritory and reached the allied lines. On reaching America he wrote a book and lectured on his experiences.

CAUSE OF DEATH
Opposing Evidence

SUICIDE	MURDER
Suicide note	Pat's sister Clara says not in his handwriting
Coroner's reports indicate suicide	Undertaker in Momence says murder
Frustration with Virginia & Sarah Ottis	Ability to overcome situations all his life
Bullet to head self-inflicted	No powder burns on wound
Post-Traumatic Syndrome	Few signs of this for three years
Stress over money losses	Had $150,000 one year before death
Newspapers reported suicide	Newspapers reported murdered
Officials determined suicide twice	Same detective used both times
Newspapers worldwide reported suicide	Virgil Moore vehemently denies
His business failures depressed him	Clara reports he spoke positively at end
Grief over Raney and others	Russian trip was a time to heal
Dr. Seager states Pat was weak from war	Little evidence prior to final days
Preponderance of press state suicide	Nearly all reports quote Sarah Ottis
Married Virginia after two weeks	Reports Pat sought Agnes at the end
Ashamed on the brevity of his service	Speeches and Uniform no sign of this
Gave up at the end	Not logical based on his lifetime of hope

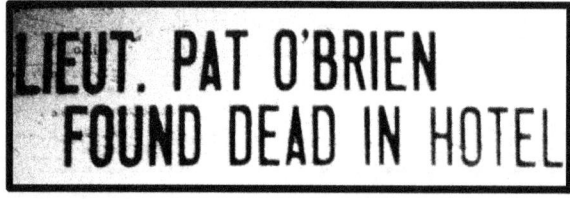

Murder

The American public had "suicide" emblazoned in its collective consciousness, until sister Clara stepped forward ten days later to declare that he was murdered.

Clara stated that the suicide letter left behind by Pat was not in his writing. She reported how Momence undertaker Melvey, after examining Pat's body, stated Pat could not have killed himself based the location of the wound and lack of powder burns near the wound, a fact that would eliminate firing at close range.

Virgil Moore, Pat's longtime friend, stated that a small "gang" of people had been stalking Pat for some time seeking his money. He also told police how he had once wrestled a pistol from "a woman" who had tried to kill Pat on four different occasions. He went on to tell of the hatred between Pat and Ottis and how Ottis had spent such large sums of Pat's money since moving in with the O'Brien's.

Conflicting evidence reported from the crime scene, including three different reports on the location of the bullet wound, added to the theory that Pat was murdered.

A central focus in nearly every report about Pat's death was the "suicide note" police and others stated was left behind by Pat. Yet, Clara stated it was not in his handwriting.

The Case for Murder

FRIEND BLAMES 'GANG PLOT' FOR DEATH OF PAT O'BRIEN; FAMILY DEMANDS INQUIRY

(By New York Times-Chicago Tribune Special Leased Wire. Copyrighted.)

LOS ANGELES, Dec. 29.—That Lieut. Pat O'Brien, who ended his own life in a room in the Alexandria Hotel here Friday night, was the victim of a conspiracy of some kind which had reduced him to poverty, caused his wife to leave him and finally broken him down mentally and physically, is the theory of Virgil Moore, aviator, and closest friend of the dead war hero.

"I know the story from start to finish," said Moore tonight in his offices in the L. W. Helman building, "and I know that if someone did not actually fire the shot that killed Pat there were several someones who pulled off some mysterious game that I could never figure, which had him in fear of something he never would tell about."

"Can you imagine Pat O'Brien being afraid of anything?" asked Moore. "Yet, I have seen him on his knees at his wife's feet, begging her to 'release him.' He told me time and again that 'gang got all his money and was making his life miserable.' I know that a year ago he had fully $150,000, that he came to Los Angeles early in the Summer with at least $10,000, and I know that within a month he didn't have a cent.

"There have been some stories printed about this whole thing and all from those who are not friendly to Pat. I only want to say a few things on his side."

According to Moore, O'Brien came to California in the hope of getting away from the acquaintances he had made in the Eastern States and Cuba and intended to marry a young woman who was supposed to have been waiting here for him.

Conspiracy Charged.

"For some unknown reason," said Moore, "he completely lost his head over a woman named Elizabeth Greene he had met in Cuba. They were married less than a year ago and were all right for a short time. It is a long story about the coming of Mrs. Sarah Otis, formerly the wife of a man in Springfield, Ill. She had met Pat during one of the Liberty Loan drives in Chicago and soon found him after she and her daughter came to Los Angeles.

"Soon after she came the daughter was married and after trouble with the daughter's husband they went to the O'Brien home to live. This was when Pat had a fine place at 2514 North Commonwealth Street. Then the trouble started. Mrs. Otis liked a lot of wild parties and seemed to have a lot of influence over Mrs. O'Brien. I was out there many a night and it was always a wild time. Things got so bad that Pat asked Mrs. Otis to get an apartment for herself, but she refused. Then came more stormy days and Pat didn't have rent money and had to move. He was here in my office when they arrived and served him with papers to get out within three days. I went out and helped them to pack up and they moved to 201 North Rampart Street. Pat's sister came out to visit him and can back up every word I am telling you. These parties kept up and more trouble followed. Finally, the last part of the tragic story was begun on Dec. 13, Pat's birthday. Mrs. Otis had framed a party at the Alexandria and insisted on Mrs. O'Brien going, but only asked Pat in a half hearted way. He stayed home with his sister and cousin. About 2 o'clock the next morning, Thursday, the two women came in, both hilarious. Then it was Pat got up enough nerve to talk turkey to Mrs Otis. He told her to pack and leave that night. She ran screaming from the house. Pat

(CONTINUED ON PAGE 3)

O'BRIEN VICTIM OF "GUN PLOT," FRIEND CHARGES

(CONTINUED FROM PAGE 1)

was afraid something awful might happen. Pat brought her back to the house. Mrs. O'Brien told Mrs. Otis, 'You better go before he kills you.'

Women Leave Home.

"They threatened to call the police and Pat gave them the telephone number. Two officers came out and told the women they had better go to bed and be quiet. Instead they waited until the police went away and then both left.

"Pat stayed at home all day Tuesday and Wednesday and came up to see me Thursday. He said he had been trying to find me to talk matters over. He seemed kind of dazed and said he couldn't find his wife. He finally located her at a doctor's office from the telephone in my office but when he got over there she was gone. I didn't see Pat again until 5 o'clock Friday afternoon when he came up here and said the gang had got all his money and had now stolen his wife. He said they were staying at the Alexandria and he was going over there and get things straightened. He engaged a room over my phone and I left him at the door of the hotel about 7 o'clock."

Moore said he didn't think anything very serious would happen and did not learn of the tragedy until he saw the headlines of a morning paper.

"I beat it to the hotel as fast as I could," said Moore.

"Finally I got upstairs to the room where the women were. All three were in bed yet when I got there. They told me the same story that has been printed in all the papers. None of them seemed to be sorry for poor Pat and all said that they didn't think he would kill himself."

Virgil Moore was in the Signal Corps with Pat and managed a portion of his speaking appearances in 1918

Pat O'Brien Murdered, Sister Now Declares

O'BRIEN SLAIN, RELATIVES SAY; DEMAND INQUIRY

Woman's Threats to Kill Aviator Recalled As Singular Circumstances In Case Undergo Investigation.

Chicago, Jan. 8.—Claiming to have gathered sufficient evidence to prove that Lieut. Pat O'Brien of Momence, Ill., famous war aviator, found shot to death in a Los Angeles hotel two weeks ago, did not die by his own hand, but fell a victim to a cleverly executed murder, relatives of the airman announced yesterday they will demand a thorough investigation of the case by the California authorities.

Ever since the flyer's death a private inquiry has been quietly conducted in Los Angeles, it was disclosed yesterday, by Merwin ("Jack") O'Brien, a brother, and pals, who served with Lieut. O'Brien as a member of the British secret service during the war. The high lights of this investigation were revealed at Momence by Lieut. O'Brien's sister, Mrs. Clara Clegg, who was with him until a few hours before his death and who accompanied the body to Momence, where it was buried Monday.

No Inquest Is Held.

No inquest was held, as the coroner expressed himself as "convinced O'Brien killed himself." The Los Angeles authorities stated that as far as they are concerned the case is "closed", but Chief of Police Pendegast offered to lend the assistance of his department in conducting any further inquiry the facts might warrant.

Relatives of the dead aviator

Continued On Page 12

O'BRIEN SLAIN, RELATIVES SAY; DEMAND INQUIRY.

Continued From Page 5.

point to the following unusual circumstances which they believe precludes the possibility of a suicide theory:

Lieut. O'Brien was in a gay mood as he talked to Mrs. Clegg five hours before his death. He spoke of aviation stunts which he intended "pulling" for the movies.

There were no powder marks on the bullet wound in his right temple.

His body was first discovered at 8 o'clock in the evening by a woman. Mrs. Clegg was not notified

Lieut. Pat O'Brien.

Relatives and friends of Lieut. Pat O'Brien, war hero, refuse to believe that he wrote his own death note and then committed suicide in a Los Angeles, Cal., hotel room, December 18. They have started an investigation of the hero's death. First reports of O'Brien's death said he shot himself because he was temporarily mentally unbalanced. His relatives say he had been threatened with death four times.

of his death until 11 o'clock, three hours later.

Lieut. O'Brien had been threatened with death by a woman on four different occasions. On one occasion, Virgil Moore, associated with O'Brien in his aeroplane appearances for the movies wrested a pistol from the woman's hand.

The revolver with which Lieut. O'Brien had been shot had been removed from the scene when Mrs. Clegg arrived. The weapon shown to her later was not the property of Lieut. O'Brien, she says.

Asserts Letter Is Not O'Brien's.

Mrs. Clegg also claims the death note, supposedly written by Lieut. O'Brien, blaming a woman for having broken up his life, was not written by her brother. She believes it was written by his slayer to "cover up" the crime.

"My boy did not commit suicide and I refuse to believe it", said Mrs. Maggie O'Brien, the heartbroken mother, to a press representative. "If he had shot himself with that gun of his it would have blown the whole top of his head off. It was a long gun, an army .48 I think he called it".

Dr. George Cole, house physician at the Hotel Alexandria where the shooting occurred, declared there is abundant proof in the hands of the coroner that Lieut. O'Brien ended his own life. Dr. Cole was one of the first to reach O'Brien's room. Dr. Howard Seager of Los Angeles, a personal friend of Lieut. O'Brien, also declared there could be no doubt the aviator committed suicide.

O'Brien Murdered, Says His Sister

MOMENCE, Ill., Dec. 28.—Lieutenant Pat O'Brien did not die a suicide on December 17 in his room in a Los Angeles hotel, but was murdered.

This was the word given out today by Mrs. Clara Clegg of this city, sister of the dead aviator, in an interview to newspapermen. Mrs. Clegg said that relatives and friends of O'Brien are insisting upon a more thorough investigation of the circumstances surrounding his death.

According to Mrs. Clegg, friends and relatives of O'Brien rely upon the following testimony in their demands:

That Lieutenant O'Brien was threatened with death by a woman on four different occasions.

That Virgil Moore, an aviator friend of O'Brien's, once wrested a pistol from this woman as she sought to fire at O'Brien.

That Pat O'Brien did not write the death note found near his body and that the note was written by the slayer to make it appear that O'Brien was mentally unbalanced.

That there were no powder stains or marks found about the wound.

Oakland Tribune

Though the District Attorney in Los Angeles is "positive" Pat's death was the result of suicide, his statement that the Pat was shot through the mouth and the bullet entered the rear wall behind Pat was countered by the undertaker who examined Pat's body and stated the bullet entered the right temple.

DECEMBER 29, 1920.
HERO MURDERED, THEY SAY.

Lieut. Pat O'Brien's Relatives Allege Woman Killed Him.

(Special to The World.)

MOMENCE, Ill., Dec. 28.—Relatives and friends of Lieut. Pat O'Brien, hero aviator, are not satisfied with the verdict of suicide rendered by the Coroner's Jury in Los Angeles, where he was supposed to have shot himself.

Mrs. Clara Clagg, his sister, and his brother have begun an investigation in which they will be assisted by all his friends.

Efforts will be made to reopen the inquiry, when, O'Brien's relatives say, they will give the authorities the name of the woman they charged killed O'Brien.

New York World Newspaper

Los Angeles Authorities Positive It Was Suicide.

(Special to The World.)

LOS ANGELES, Dec. 28.—The police, the Coroner's office and the District Attorney's office to-night expressed their conviction that Lieut. Pat O'Brien killed himself. The aviator-hero was shot through the mouth, the bullet passing out and piercing the wall near the ceiling. The angle at which the bullet struck the wall, officials say, is proof conclusive that no one but O'Brien himself could have fired the shot.

The District Attorney declared his willingness to thoroughly investigate any evidence tending to disprove suicide that may be presented to him.

Evidence shot was fired "from a distance"

Autopsy not performed until Pat's body returns to Momence. Newspaper reports based on the L.A.P.D. detective that performed the 1st & 2nd investigation.

Undertaker Melvey declared "no powder marks or burns about the wound" would indicated shot was fired "some distance" from Pat's head.

MURDER, NOT SUICIDE.

Such Now Appears to Have Caused Lieut. O'Brien's Death.

Momence, Ill., Dec. 29.—Further evidence that Lieut. Pat O'Brien, aviator, who died in his room in a Los Angeles hotel Dec. 17, did not commit suicide, but was killed by a shot fired from a distance, was elicited today from J. E. Melvey, undertaker, who made a careful examination of the body upon its arrival here for burial a few days ago.

Questioned by relatives of O'Brien, who are determined upon further investigation of the former birdman's death, Melvey declared today that there were no powder marks or burns about the wound and that the shot must have been fired from "some distance."

Contrary to the statements of Los Angeles authorities yesterday and at the time of Lieut. O'Brien's death, Melvey declared that O'Brien had not been shot through the mouth and that only one bullet had taken effect and it had passed from the right temple to a point just above the hair line on the left temple.

Los Angeles police stated the gunshot was made "through the mouth." Undertaker describes wound to be "from the right temp to a point just above the hair line on the left temple"

CRIME SCENE verses AUTOPSY

PAT O'BRIEN WAS MURDERED, CLAIM FLIER'S RELATIVES

Pat O'Brien, Famous Ace, Spent His Last Hours With Air Pal

Los Angeles, Dec. 18.—(I. N. S.)—It developed today that Lieutenant Pat O'Brien, famous war aviator who killed himself in a downtown hotel late last night, had spent his last few hours with Bert Hall, an English aviator, whom he had known while in the air service during the war.

O'Brien and Hall discussed plans for a reunion dinner on Christmas day, at which they would be joined by Eddie Rickenbacker and William Thaw, all of whom were in service in the aviation corps and were comrades overseas.

Thaw is coming from Mexico now and was expected to be here in time for the contemplated Christmas reunion.

Friends of O'Brien expressed the belief that he was mentally unbalanced as a result of his battle experiences when he shot himself with an army automatic pistol following the refusal of his wife to see him.

"I was in mortal fear of Pat," said Mrs. O'Brien, "and I was afraid to live with him for fear he would take my life."

Mrs. O'Brien declared Mrs. Sarah Ottis, mentioned by O'Brien in a note written by him shortly before he shot himself as "that awful woman that has broken our home and has taken you from me," was in no way responsible for the troubles of the O'Briens.

"Mrs. Ottis was just a friend to me, more like a mother than anything else," said Mrs. O'Brien, who is prostrated over the act of her husband. Mrs. Ottis, who has been Mrs. O'Brien's companion, said the aviator had been irritational for several weeks.

SISTER ASSERTS O'BRIEN MURDERED, NOT SUICIDE

MOMENCE, Ill., Dec. 28.—Expressing her belief that her brother, Lieut. Pat O'Brien, war aviator, who was found dead in a hotel in Los Angeles two weeks ago, was murdered, Mrs. Clara Clegg said today that further investigation would be made. Mrs. Clegg said that her brother, Merwin O'Brien, and Virgil Moore, a friend, had sufficient evidence to warrant an investigation and she believed the fact would be established that O'Brien did not commit suicide.

Mrs. Clegg said she had been with Pat in the afternoon prior to the shooting and he was in good spirits and she also declared that when she saw his body there were no powder marks near the wound. She said she believed the note which was found with the body was written by some person to cover up the crime.

INVESTIGATE DEATH OF WORLD WAR HERO

(Special to The Republican.)

Los Angeles, Dec. 18.—Police are investigating the mysterious death of Lieut. Pat O'Brien, of Momence, Ill., one of the most noted heroes of the war who was found shot to death in his room in local hotel.

It is believed O'Brien shot himself because of the seperation from his wife with whom he had vainly attempted reconciliation. The possibility that O'Brien's death may have been caused by another person is being investigated.

O'BRIEN SLAIN, RELATIVES SAY; DEMAND INQUIRY

Woman's Threats to Kill Aviator Recalled As Singular Circumstances In Case Undergo Investigation.

Chicago, Jan. 8.—Claiming to have gathered sufficient evidence to prove that Lieut. Pat O'Brien of Momence, Ill., famous war aviator, found shot to death in a Los Angeles hotel two weeks ago, did not die by his own hand, but fell a victim to a cleverly executed murder, relatives of the airman announced yesterday they will demand a thorough investigation of the case by the California authorities.

Ever since the flyer's death a private inquiry has been quietly conducted in Los Angeles, it was disclosed yesterday, by Merwin ("Jack") O'Brien, a brother, and pals, who served with Lieut. O'Brien as a member of the British secret service during the war. The high lights of this investigation were revealed at Momence by Lieut. O'Brien's sister, Mrs. Clara Clegg, who was with him until a few hours before his death and who accompanied the body to Momence, where it was buried Monday.

No Inquest Is Held.

No inquest was held, as the coroner expressed himself as "convinced O'Brien killed himself." The Los Angeles authorities stated that as far as they are concerned the case is "closed", but Chief of Police Pendegast offered to lend the assistance of his department in conducting any further inquiry the facts might warrant.

Relatives of the dead aviator point to the following unusual circumstances which they believe precludes the possibility of a suicide theory:

Lieut. O'Brien was in a gay mood as he talked to Mrs. Clegg five hours before his death. He spoke of aviation stunts which he intended "pulling" for the movies.

There were no powder marks on the bullet wound in his right temple.

His body was first discovered at 8 o'clock in the evening by a woman. Mrs. Clegg was not notified of his death until 11 o'clock, three hours later.

Lieut. O'Brien had been threatened with death by a woman on four different occasions. On one occasion, Virgil Moore, associated with O'Brien in his aeroplane appearances for the movies wrested a pistol from the woman's hand.

The revolver with which Lieut. O'Brien had been shot had been removed from the scene when Mrs. Clegg arrived. The weapon shown to her later was not the property of Lieut. O'Brien, she says.

Asserts Letter Is Not O'Brien's.

Mrs. Clegg also claims the death note, supposedly written by Lieut. O'Brien, blaming a woman for having broken up his life, was not written by her brother. She believes it was written by his slayer to "cover up" the crime.

"My boy did not commit suicide and I refuse to believe it", said Mrs. Maggie O'Brien, the heartbroken mother, to a press representative. "If he had shot himself with that gun of his it would have blown the whole top of his head off. It was a long gun, an army .48 I think he called it".

Dr. George Cole, house physician at the Hotel Alexandria where the shooting occurred, declared there is abundant proof in the hands of the coroner that Lieut. O'Brien ended his own life. Dr. Cole was one of the first to reach O'Brien's room. Dr. Howard Seager of Los Angeles, a personal friend of Lieut. O'Brien, also declared there could be no doubt the aviator committed suicide.

The debate surrounding

Pat O'Brien's death...

THE CASE FOR SUICIDE

Evidence to support the theory that Pat O'Brien took his own life falls into two categories: Pat's psychological state at the time of his death, and the physical evidence reported to be at the "crime scene."

Pat's Mental State

Los Angeles police detectives, Sarah Ottis, Virginia and Dr. Walter Seager, who the newspapers described as "Pat's physician and friend." all made statements to the press that they believed Pat took his own life. Virginia and Sarah Ottis stated that they believed Pat suffered from a "psychosis" relating to his war experience. Seager told the papers that Pat suffered from a "wrecked nervous equilibrium" at the time of his death. Other reports pointed to Pat's likely depression over failed projects and financial depletion.

Pat could have been impacted psychologically by his experiences in the war. Those who suspect he suffered from what is now known as post-traumatic syndrome point to the likely impact of combat on his mental state, the loss of his close friend Paul Raney, his possible guilt over having served for a short time and his unsuccessful efforts to rejoin the war in atonement for his self-perceived inadequate service. Pat did believe he made a minimal contribution as compared to nearly every pilot in his Canadian group, "the original 18," who entered the Royal Flying Corp and died in action.

At the time of World War I, little was known about the psychological impact of war. Two million soldiers fought in the war and 159,000 were put out of action for psychiatric reasons. At the time, psychological symptoms centered on what was then called "shell shock." Shell shock included stuttering, crying, trembling, paralysis, stupor and other disorders. Long term or latent effects of war were basically unknown to the military. Knowing what we know today, one might conclude that Pat had latent reactions to the psychological effects of war, contributing to his self-demise.

It would be reasonable to conclude that Pat was not given enough time to unwind following his ordeal. His book writing began while still recovering in London and he signed his speaking tour contract in New York even before he arrived back home in Momence. He began making speeches almost immediately, toured for over a year and never seemed to take time to recover from war or his traumatic escape. His busy touring could have delayed his reconciliation with war's effects yet he died nearly two years after his escape. His trip to Russia in 1919 could be viewed as his attempt to atone for his perceived "short service" but little is known about his motivations.

A second psychological theory hinges on Pat's unprecedented and sudden loss of money, success and his break-up with Agnes in 1919. It seems apparent that though Pat was unwilling to give up his trip to Russia and marry Agnes, he made that choice expecting to return and start a life with her. His behavior certainly took a turn once she broke off the relationship. The complications surrounding "Shadows of the West" and failed investments in other projects such as the Allen Car dealership would certainly wear down even the strongest among us. His sudden and uncharacteristic marriage to Virginia seems as impulsive as his trip to Siberia. But both are symptoms rather than causes of his state of mind and, perhaps, his eventual suicide.

In the end, we can only speculate about the inner feelings and thoughts Pat possessed upon his death. Indeed, those present when he died would have little more understanding than we as to what was motivating him at the end of his life. Possessing only speculation and nebulous evidence, one may turn to the physical evidence found at the scene. Unfortunately, much of that is also vague, contradictory and incomplete.

Physical Evidence

The physical evidence supporting suicide as the cause of Pat's death would be more clear-cut if it were not for conflicting evidence in the newspapers, in statements by police, from hotel employees present that night and from people who saw Pat in the last week of his life.

If one believes that police departments used adequate investigative methods in 1920, which they did not, more credibility could be placed in their reports. Pat killed himself around 2:30 a.m. on December 18, 1920 and police detectives filed their report, concluding Pat killed himself around 1:00 p.m. that afternoon following an "investigation." There were conflicting newspaper reports on the time of Pat's death but newspapers do get things wrong and, as best we can determine he died in the early hours of the December 18.

Nearly all information acquired by the police regarding events leading up to Pat's death came from Sarah Ottis. A week later, after reports were filed, Pat's friend, Virgil Moore and Pat's sister Clara told the press conflicting information about Pat's last day. Clara had taken Pat's body home. But Merwin stayed behind and with the help of Virgil and others, tried to uncover some facts and also find Pat's money. Sarah Ottis and Virginia were not helpful. In fact, Virginia, technically, Merwin's sister-in-law, would not see him.

The Los Angeles Police concluded that Pat killed himself with the army pistol found "at his side." Newspapers in Los Angles, however, reported different facts regarding the location of the wound. One reported Pat shot himself in the forehead, another indicated he shot himself in the mouth and the bullet exited out the back of his head and a third stated he shot himself in the temple. J. E. Molvey, the undertaker in Momence, admittedly someone who might have an interest in disproving police reports, stated emphatically that the bullet could not have been fired by Pat since there was "no sign of gun power surrounding the wound." This, he said, would indicate that Pat was shot "at a distance." Upon completing his autopsy back in Momence, he stated that the bullet entered Pat's head at the hairline of the temple and exited out the right side of the head. It is not known if Pat was right or left handed.

A second focus of physical evidence was the famous "suicide note" left behind by Pat where he expressed his despondency over his marital troubles and belittled himself as a quitter in a hopeless situation. Police reported the "suicide note" as additional proof Pat killed himself but Pat's sister Clara would later purport that it was not in Pat's handwriting.

He pointed to the "awful woman" who had such a negative effect on his wife. He stated that she ruined his marriage.

Molvey's report spurred appeals from the O'Brien family for a formal inquiry. At first they were denied but pressure from family, friends and a number of people associated with the film industry result in two inquiries that reached the same conclusion.

There was evidence that Sarah Ottis and Virginia influenced public and police opinion regarding Pat's death. Police to official statements from hotel staff but their primary source of information was Sarah Ottis who presented herself as a spokesperson for the family. She is quoted extensively about the events of Pat's last day, providing a timetable for police and newspaper reporters. Virginia was notably absent. Only one short interview could be found in the press with Virginia a few days after Pat's death.

Virginia made one statement and both women disappeared from all news within a week. Sarah Ottis stated emphatically that he had been violent in recent weeks and strongly connected her allegation to the likely effects of war.

But the convincing item that was front and center in all newspaper reports was the suicide note purported to be written by Pat. It clearly set public opinion though denied by the O'Brien family. Until further proof is found a good number shall conclude he killed himself.

Police state their initial findings are correct and that no further inquiry to Pat's death will be made. Under pressure from the O'Briens and Pat's friends, they later agree to investigate. They duplicate their first inquiry and add their opinion as to Pat's motivations (war depression) as promoted by Sarah Ottis, Virginia and Dr. Seager. This would be considered highly speculative today.

Lieut. O'Brien Hero of Five Wars, Kills Self; "I'm Coward" Says Note

THE CASE FOR MURDER

If Pat was murdered it would not have been a random act. If it were a robbery, for example, there would be no suicide note, nor any reason for anyone to write one. Therefore, if Pat did not kill himself, then it must be concluded that he was murdered as part of a conspiratorial plan, either for hate (perhaps in the case of Sarah Ottis), envy (as could be the case with Virginia) or money (which could include any number of people acting individually or as a group).

Evidence that suggests Pat could have been murdered falls into three categories. Newspaper statements that conflict or sound suspicious coming from certain people, conflicting physical evidence that is hard to dismiss as a technical misstatement, and the actions of Sarah Ottis and Virginia Dale following Pat's death that could hardly be classified as coming from mourners.

There is a fourth gnawing reason that causes murder-conspiracy theorists to doubt Pat O'Brien killed himself. It is the highly unlikely scenario that a man, who was the epitome of optimism and the "never give up spirit," throughout his life, could fall into such deep despair at the end of his life - regardless of his war experiences. After all, Pat opened his book ""Outwitting the Hun" with the chapter entitled, "The Folly of Despair."

Nebulous Newspaper Reports

Nearly all of the information on the death of Pat used for the book "Lt. Pat O'Brien" comes from newspaper reports. As of this publication, no one has seen the actual detective files which may still be in the Los Angeles Police Department archives. There are plans to do more research.

During Pat's time, all news was distributed via the newspaper. As with the Associated Press and other services today, one story was written locally and wired to hundreds of news outlets throughout the country. Three primary Los Angeles-based newspapers published variations of Pat's demise. One focused extensively on the suicide note, another quoted statements for Sarah Ottis and the third speculated about Pat and Virginia's troubled marriage. With few exceptions, most newspapers across the country published one of these three reports. Little of the formal investigation details were reported in any of these local newspaper reports or in wire reports.

Dominance of Suicide Stories

In the first week following Pat's death, news reports unanimously declared that the cause of death was suicide. In addition, the first wire story issued from California was reprinted in many newspapers around the country, all reporting suicide and all detailing the existence of a suicide note. But so much of this theory was based on extensive statements given to the press by Sarah Ottis. The O'Brien family and those who knew him, never believed it. The family and most people in Momence who know Pat's history do not believe it today. It was a week before Clara gave a statement to the press that the family suspected murder. Following her statement, pressure built on the Los Angeles Police Department to conduct a second inquiry, which they did. By that time, however, the American public had concluded Pat committed suicide and the second inquiry drew the same conclusion.

The Suicide Note

The "suicide note" left behind by Pat was quoted many times in news reports. The police stated further that there were "many" notes left behind by Pat. The primary suicide note was, as best we can tell, quoted verbatim in the press. A number of things stand out. Assuming Pat wrote the letter he states that it was Sarah Ottis who caused his demise, ruined his marriage and took his money. He says nothing negative about Virginia. He states that he is a mere man, "of clay" and a "coward," for what he is about to do. Reading this note, it is difficult to imagine this being the same man who opened his book "Outwitting the Hun" with a chapter entitled "The Folly of Despair." Everything one reads about Pat and everything thing he did his entire life up until this suicide note points to an exceptional person who would have not considered ending his life.

Those who believe the suicide note is bogus (and Clara stated to the press that it was not in Pat's handwriting), conclude that Sarah Ottis contrived the note. At first glance this may be rejected since the note contains such accusatory comments toward Sarah herself. What better way, however, to divert attention away from Sarah by accusing herself in the note of causing the discourse in the O'Brien household.

Conflicting Evidence

Inconsistent forensic reports

Three local Los Angeles newspapers reported the location of Pat's wound in three different places. It was reported he was shot 1) in the temple, 2) in his mouth and 3) in the forehead. Did reporters get it wrong or did detectives give our bogus information? Where did the newspapers get this information? Was it word of mouth? The undertaker back in Momence located the wound in the fourth location, stating that Pat was shot near the hairline and that there were no powder burns on the wound, something that would have made a self-inflicted gunshot impossible. He went on to state to the press that Pat could not have been shot at close range.

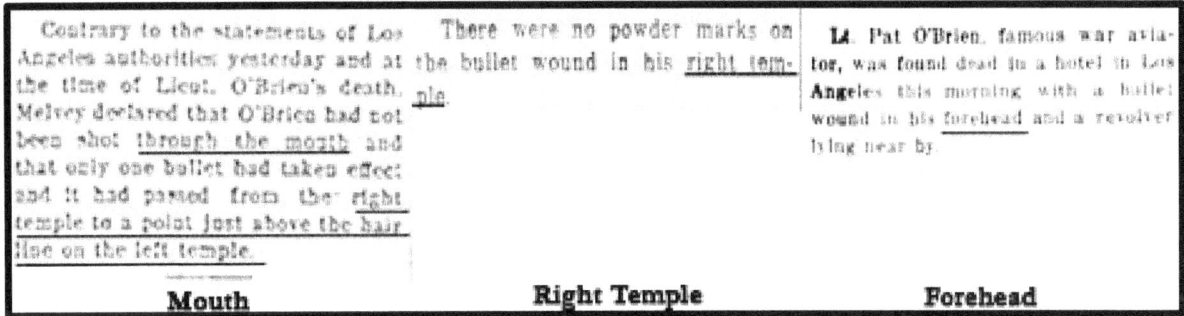

Some newspapers reported Pat was found with "a gun in his hand." Another stated it was "by his side." Both seem a bit farfetched, particularly the report of Pat holding his own suicide weapon, since it would have surely fell from his hand and likely to the floor once fired.

Weak and conflicting investigation

Stories in the newspaper gave the strong impression that much of what the police department concluded was based on the suicide note and statements given to the police by Sarah Ottis. When the undertaker in Momence reported that Pat could not have been shot from close range, due to the lack of powered burns on the wound and the location of the wound (different from official police reports) the Los Angeles police department defended its "scientific" investigation by referring to the suicide note. Officials stated that "despite conflicting reports regarding the location of the wound," the presence of the suicide note convinced them that Pat had killed himself.

Pat's lost fortune

Clara headed back to Momence with Pat's body while Merwin stayed behind to figure out what had happened and what had become of Pat's money and possessions. Virgil Moore and other friends helped Merwin piece together some facts but it was at least a week before any new stories appeared casting doubt on Pat's death by suicide. Merwin could not find a dime of Pat's money. Sarah was not forthcoming, hiding behind the notion that she was "just a family friend," and Virginia would not meet with Merwin and to our knowledge, never did. Pat's mother had little money at the end of her life and Clara died penniless in the Wilmington, Illinois Soldiers and Sailors Home.

Motivations of Sarah, Virginia and others

Reported Marital Troubles

Pat's marriage to Virginia is somewhat unusual if for no other reason than the two-week courtship which preceded it. This is the first sign that Pat may not have been thinking straight upon his return from Russia. But it is clear that he loved Agnes MacMillan and her rejection of him upon his return from Siberia may have set Pat spinning. Though a debutante, Virginia would be considered a woman of independence. She was a reporter in Washington DC who fought to get significant stories to write about. It is unlikely that she would not have an active role in pursuing Pat. Pat was about to sign a contract for a movie deal and Virginia had been unsuccessfully pursuing a starlet career for one year. She traveled with Pat to Cuba and when they returned they were man and wife.

Those who believe there was a plot to kill Pat believe that it began with Sarah and Virginia, joined by others they recruited, as stated by Virgil Moore, Pat's close friend. Whether it began with Sarah or Virginia is irrelevant but they would have worked together to get Pat married to Virginia, allow Virginia into Pat's movie picture (which she was) and eventually spend all his money or a good portion of it before he died "of his own hand." Virginia could have had an additional motive at the end as U.S. censors cut the size of Pat's film from eight to five reels, eliminating all of Virginia's appearances in the film. We may never know if these two women conspired against Pat but clearly their activities while he was alive were brash if not conspiratorial. They accused Pat of hitting and fighting with Virginia at the end. A bit hard to believe based on Pat's life but the profile of Pat as a mad villain at the end of his life would have fit their purposes. Paragraph after paragraph about this "soap opera" appeared in many news reports, proving that newspapers back in 1920 knew how to sell papers.

Sarah Ottis

No other character in the story of "Lt. Pat O'Brien" is more mysterious than Sarah Ottis. Sarah met Pat for the first time within a week of his return to Momence. Pat spoke at Orchestra Hall in Chicago and she was there. Pat appeared at a number of bond drives and fund-raisers for the war and Sarah was frequently at the same events.

She had recently divorced her husband Daniel Mortimer Ottis who was quite famous in his own right being one of Sherman's medical staff. She was older than Pat so it doesn't seem likely that she was attracted to him personally but was clearly attracted to his fame and eventual fortune. Sarah shows all indication of being a social climber and someone who liked being among the influential. With her husband's departure, she likely saw Pat as a vehicle to society. Pat was a very popular and well-known war hero and she perceived that immediately. Sarah Ottis and Virginia made a great team. Both were motivated by fame one being society's upper echelons and the other to be a movie star, something that every young girl of the time dreamed of each day. The authors believe Pat walked into the mob world of Arnold Rothstein "wide-eyed." It's likely he may have done the same when he entered the realm of Sarah Ottis and Virginia Dale, both highly motivated

The Essence of Pat O'Brien

Finally, one comes away from the story of Pat O'Brien with more questions than answers. Even after seven-plus years of research the authors of this book lean in different directions when it comes to the cause of Pat's death. Marcia Tedford believes that the war's effect, the loss of Agnes and the tumultuous year of 1920 finally became too much for Pat. Pat had very little downtime after his war. He was a public figure the day he arrived in Momence and began speaking all around the United States. Kevin McNulty believed Pat's trip to Russia was his "40 days in the desert" and was the first time Pat had time to slow down and perhaps, reflect. He leans more in the direction of murder. No one knows what words were spoken between Pat and Agnes prior to his departure for Russia but the break-up could have occurred then. If so, Pat's trip to Russia could have been a stew that festered rather than a retreat that rejuvenated him. Clearly, Pat did not visit Agnes upon his return and went immediately out to New York. There he fell into the seedy world of mob boss Arnold Rothstein. In less than a year he would marry Virginia.

All reports from Pat's hometown of Momence and from his decedents indicate that Pat was a highly energetic, independent risk-taking child. His teachers described him as lovable yet mischievous. He clearly was not the typical child. He was special. He was not the typical man either as demonstrated by his pursuit of flying and his determined escape from German hands. The reserve of determination that a man would need to pursue seventy-two days in hiding, living on the land and overcoming obstacles that would stop even the above average person, is uncanny. No doubt the night his captives discovered him full of lice, the time he swam a river at its bend and swam a second time arriving where he first started or watched as his buddy Paul Raney fall from the sky required a strength reserved for few men. No one will ever know what was on the mind of Pat O'Brien in his final days on this earth but his life of thirty years is a legacy unmatched many.

Part X
Legacy

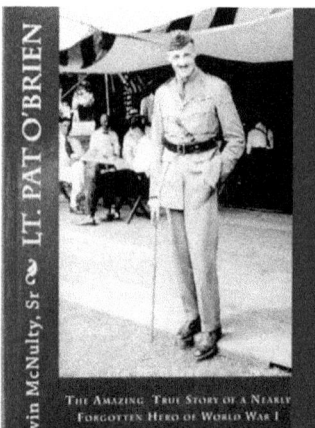

Chapter Reference

PART X ~ Legacy

Corresponding Chapters in "Lt. Pat O'Brien"

Chapter 55 Last Train Home   772

PART XII EPILOGUE   785

Legacy ~ Even if you had never seen photo of Pat O'Brien but knew of his life, would there be any doubt in the above photo who is Pat? He appears above leaning on the fuselage of plane flashing that famous mug that earned him the nickname "Smiling Pat." What none of us today can appreciate, that only those that knew him could, is the dynamic and charismatic personality of this "bigger-than-life" hero that inspired millions of Americans, Canadians and Europeans that lived in his time.

To those who watched him grow up in Momence it must have been a thrill to see him at his loftiest peak and crushing to experience his lowest ebb as his body was laid to rest in the Momence Cemetery. He lies their today, finally with an appropriate marker placed in 2007 by citizens of Momence. Either through shame or the mere fact that Margaret could not afford a stone for Pat, his burial place was unmarked and went unknown by most for eighty-seven years. It is a tribute to Pat's greatness that he was not forgotten. It is also a tribute to the people of Momence who never forgot how important he was. There are few small towns in American with a love and respect for their history as is the people of Momence.

Before the tragic end of Pat O'Brien's life, Momence was a hearty town that believed it could do anything. After Pat's death, Momence understood that "what goes up," no matter how high, can always "come down."

NO BAND, NO PARADE GREETS DEAD HERO.

BODY OF PAT O'BRIEN REACHES OLD HOME—NOTED FLIER TO BE BURIED MONDAY.

[EXCLUSIVE DISPATCH]

CHICAGO, Dec. 23.—Less than two years ago Mrs Margaret O'Brien and virtually all the population of Momence, Ill., assembled at the railway station to welcome Lieut. Pat O'Brien, war aviator extraordinary. There was a brass band and speeches and a great community dinner in the City Hall and a street parade and Mrs Margaret O'Brien's heart swelled with pride almost to the bursting point.

This evening another crowd assembled at the station, but there was no band, no parade and no cheers It met the body of O'Brien, who killed himself in Los Angeles. The remains were accompanied by Mrs Clara Clegg, a married sister who had been visiting him in California.

O'Brien shot himself, leaving a note telling of his failure to effect a reconciliation with his wife and referring vaguely to another woman who had caused the trouble

He will be buried Monday. Momence will speedily forget his suicide, but the memory of his daring deeds and miraculous escapes will be cherished in the little city's history and passed down to future generations.

PAT O'BRIEN'S OLD FRIENDS HONOR HIM

MOMENCE, Ill., Dec. 24.—The body of Lieut. Pat. O'Brien, aviator who won honors in the world war, arrived from Los Angeles, where he committed suicide. The station platform was crowded with sorrowing friends of the flier who two years ago arrived to receive their praise for his exploits overseas. His mother, Mrs. Margaret O'Brien, was unable to go to the station because of an indisposition.

PAT O'BRIEN BURIED

By Associated Press.

MOMENCE, Ill., Dec. 27.—Funeral services were held today in his boyhood home for Lieut. Patrick O'Brien, formerly of the Royal British Flying corps, who killed himself at Los Angeles last week after failing to obtain reconciliation with his wife.

Aviator Brought Home

Momence, Ill., Dec. 24—Pat O'Brien was back to this sleepy little village he left many years ago to start on his picturesque career, during which he fought in six wars and was decorated by two kings.

The body of the American flyer who killed himself in Los Angeles because his wife, a movie star, refused to return to him, arrived here today. The funeral will be held Monday.

Momence Press Reporter Momence, Illinois
Friday, December 31, 1920

FUNERAL OF LIEUT. O'BRIEN ON MONDAY

IMPRESSIVE SERVICES HELD AT THE CHURCH AND CEMETERY

WAS LARGELY ATTENDED

A REPRESENTATIVE OF THE BRITISH ARMY
SENT TO ATTEND THE SERVICES

Momence paid its last tribute to its world-famed war hero on Monday morning. Momence honored Lieutenant Pat. Alva O'Brien in life, and paid its last homage at his funeral. Never before in the history of this city has such showers of sympathy, love and esteem been bestowed upon on of its citizens.

While his friends were lamenting the tragic ending of the life which had so meant much to the world, the United States, England, the state of Illinois and Kankakee county, they stopped their life's activities long enough to pay honor to the distinguished soldier.

While the entire world mourns the death of Pat O' Brien it was Momence, where he was known to every man, woman and child that the blow fell the heaviest. Those who had known him since the days that he was barefooted boy here, and who watched with admiration his eventful career from the time he entered the war, through his thrilling experience. In Germany, the bestowing upon him of the highest military honors, on Monday stood with bowed heads and sad hearts, while the final chapter in that life was brought to an end. Even closer than to all others fell the terrible blow on the aged mother. She it was who watched with a loving heart and just pride the career of her boy, and to her the blow was one that only a mother can realize.

Owing to the fact the train which brought Capt. Brandt the representative of the British and Canadian armies to the funeral was late the services were delayed about an hour, and it was about eleven o'clock before procession left the home.

The procession was headed by about fifty ex- service men. Following came the Masons of which about 75 were in line. Then came the hearse bearing the body, surrounded by the active pallbearers, honorary pallbearers and the Knight Templar escort of honor. Then followed the relatives and friends in automobiles, and it was estimated that nearly one hundred in machines were in line. Long before the cortege arrived at the church, every available seat was taken. Seats had been reserved for the family and organization represented. It was one of the largest congregations ever assembled in the church. The music was furnished by a quartet composed of Mr. and Mrs. I. E. Hardy, Miss Mabel Sergeant and Will Ward. During the service Miss Sergeant sang "Face to Face" which was one of the favorites of the deceased.

After the scripture and prayer, Rev. Wilson called upon Capt. Brandt, of the British army, who paid a short and glowing tribute to Pat O'Brien as a man and a soldier. Rev. Wilson preceded his sermon with a beautiful tribute to the career of Momence's hero. In his sermon he eulogized the dead, comforted the sorrowing and admonished the congregation.

At the close of the services a large number accompanied the remains to the cemetery, where the impressive ceremonies of the Masonic order were observed. O. A. Burdick acted as Master, William Lyne, chaplain, and M. C. Astle marshal.

Notwithstanding the bitter cold, none of the services were omitted, and never were they more solemnly conducted.

The home, the church and the grave were banked with flowers, the loving tribute from friends from all sections of the country.

The active pallbearers were Will Hupp, Howard Deliere, Harry Exline, George Ward, Arthur Pittman and Harry Hoag, all boyhood friends of the deceased. The honorary pallbearers were F.M. Nichols, A. S. Burtt, C. B. Astle, Ed. Green, C. L. Tabler, C. F. Schronts, Garylord Hess and L.P. Basford, all Shriners.

Those from out of town who attended the funeral were Elmer O'Brien and Mrs. E. Radtke of Morocco, Perry O' Brien and wife, Mrs. Wm. O'Brien, L. E. Cleaver and wife of Gary, Clarence O'Brien of Hammond, Miss Marie Worley, and Mr. & Mrs. George Bailey and Mr. and Mrs. Jack Black, Mr. and Mrs. Normanson and children and Harry Clark of Lowell, Mrs. Ed Burgess of Plymouth, Ind., Bert Ritter, Dave Alderdyce, George Diamond, and Colonel Brandt, sent to represent the British government of Chicago, Mrs. Joe McCoy of Warsaw Ind., Ross Thayer of Wisconsin, Jack Clegg of Oakland, Cal. Merwin O'Brien was detained in California, and Mrs. Ben Worley of Lowell, was unable to attend on account of illness. Ivan O'Brien who lives at home and Mrs. Clara Clegg were also in attendance.

FAMLY MEMBERS IN ATTENDANCE AT FUNERAL

MOMENCE RESIDENTS
Margaret O'Brien   Mother
Ivan O'Brien   Brother
Clara Clegg   Sister

RELATIVES FROM OUT OF TOWN

Elmer O'Brien, Brother, Morocco, IN
Mrs. Wm. O'Brien   Unknown
Clarence O'Brien, Brother, Hammond, IN
Miss Marie Worley, Sister in Law, Lowell, IN
Jack Clegg, Nephew, Oakland, CA

UNABLE TO ATTEND

Mrs. Ben Worley, Aunt, Lowell, IN
Illness

Merwin O'Brien, Brother
Detained having made arrangements for having Pat "s body to be returned to Momence. Merwin remained in California involved with an investigation of the possibility of Pat having been murdered.

"Lt. Pat O'Brien"
Timeline

1920 - December 18 - 1987 - 2007 - July 31

December 18	Buck and young Jack Clegg arrive in Los Angeles from San Francisco to join Clara.
December 18	Noon - reports arrive back at Momence of Pat's death.
December 20	Clara, Merwin and Virgil Moore hold a press conference stating Pat was murdered.
December 23	Clara and her son Jack Clegg arrive back in Momence with Pat's body.
December 27	Pat's funeral held at the Methodist Church.
January 2 (est.)	Merwin comes to Momence from Los Angeles. No sign of Pat's estate.
January 3 (est.)	Chief Lyle Prendergast of Los Angeles Police Department orders second inquiry. Results are the same.
1924	Margaret's sister Lila dies. Margaret moves back to Momence from Lowell.
1925	Margaret sends letter to Air Force Association of Canada inquiring about possible benefits
1930	Margaret Dies in her home in Momence
2007 - July 31	A group of Momence citizens hold a dedication ceremony at Momence Cemetery

LIEUT. PAT O'BRIEN LAID TO REST

Honored by Royal Blood and by the People of his own town he is laid to rest in Momence Cemetery.

(edited from original - Momence Progress, - December 30, 1920)

On Monday morning at 10:00 o'clock the Methodist church was taxed to it seating capacity with the friends of Lt. Pat O'Brien and before the sermon began standing room was at a premium. The Masons with their accustomed services were in of the casket containing the body of the deceased hero and soldier. Upon entering the sanctuary, Miss Helena Hardy presiding at the organ played the "Death March in Saul" by Handel while the funeral party was being escorted to theirs seats.

The minister read the twenty-third psalm. The quartette composed of Miss Sergeant, Mrs. IE Harry, Messrs. W.J. Ward and I.E. Hardy sang the hymns "Go bury they Sorrow" and "Abide With Me." The 39th psalm, a portion of the 14th chapter of St John's gospel and verses from the 21st chapter of Revelation were read. Prayer was offered and Miss Mabel Sergeant sang "Fare to Fare" by Herbert Johnson.

At this point the Minister Rev. D Wilson made appropriate remarks expressive of the good will that exists between the British Empire and the United States introduced the representative of His Majesty's Government the King of England, Captain D. H. Grant, of the Canadian Army who presented the condolence of the British Empire and paid a splendid tribute to his deceased comrade and friend saying that Lt. O'Brien was a heroic soldier, a manly comrade and above a devoted son to his mother and that at this service he was worth of just as much honor as he would have received had met his death in the battle overseas.

The obituary as it appeared in the Momence papers was read. As an introduction to his sermon a poem was given.

[Selected quotes from sermon]

"It may be some comfort to know that you are in the midst of friends and that your son and brother will sleep under the Momence skies and be lovingly remembered by his fellow townsmen."

"Life has a beginning but no end. There is a point of departure, where the human soul enters upon the scene of action, but no point at which it ceases to be. Human life is bounded by two dates birth and death. These however are but the bound on the leasehold that we have and the things of time."

There comes the time of departure for another habitation with an environment in keeping with the eternal sphere into which the spirit of man enters.

If I may illustrate my thought by the thing which is entirely familiar to those who were enlisted in the armies of our nation. There came a day and a time when the civilian became a soldier, when he put off daily habits, conduct and clothing of civilian life and became a soldier in the army. Clad in the garments of the Nation with a will surrendered to the will of those who had the authority to command.

The same man but a new environment. He had put off the things of the civilian life and put on the things of the soldiers life. The illustration lays emphasis upon a fact which each of us must face and hold us to a condition from which no man has ever yet escaped. At the end of our mortal day when we ceased to be a civilian in the land of the living and become a resident of eternity. The same person is in a new environment. The answer the first petition is that end of human life begins the endless life.

At the end of mortality the early assignment ceases. At the beginning of eternity eternal assignments are made by the hand of the most worth Judge Eternal, whose character is Love, whost judgments are true and righteous altogether, whose mercy is everlasting, whose knowledge is infinite. He knoweth our frame, he remembereth that we are dust. Shall not the Judge of all the earth do right? At the end of this life we become citizens of Eternity.

Lieut. O'Brien leaves to mourn his mother Mrs. Margaret O'Brien, five brothers and two sisters, who were all present at the funeral except one brother Merwin O'Brien of Oakland Calif. and Mrs. Ben Worley of Lowell Ind, who was unable to be present. Those attending the funeral from out of town were: Mr. and Mrs. Perry O'Brien, Mrs. Wm. Brien and two sons Verne and Kenard, and Mr. and Mrs. L.D. Cleaver of Gary, Ind.; Elmer O'Brien and Mrs. Elizabeth Radtke, Morocco, Ind, Clarence O'Brien Hammond, Ind, Jack Clegg, Mather Field, Calif., Miss Marie Worley, Mr. and Mrs. Geo. Baily, Mr. and Mrs. Jas. Black, Mr. and Mrs. A. Nomanson, two sons and daughter, Lowell, Ind., Ross Thayer, Dowagaic, Mich, Dave Alderdyce, Bert Ritter, Harry Clary and Geo. M Diamond Chicago, Clifford Condon, Chicago Heights.

This was the largest funeral ever accord any man in this city. Friends from all parts of the state were in attendance. Over two hundred automobiles were in the procession. First came the American Legion, the Masons followed and them the hearse and pallbearers. The honorary pallbearers were members of the Ivanhoe Commandry of Kankakee. Burial was in Momence Cemetery.

WE THANK YOU

We wish to thank our many dear friends, the lodges, the choir and Rev. Wilson for the acts of love and sympathy show us in our great bereavement. Also for the many beautiful floral designs and sprays which decorated the casket and room where our loved on the and brother slept. We thank you one and all

Mrs. Margaret O'Brien and Family.

(note appeared in Momence Progress Newspaper, following the funeral)

June 16, 1925
ACTUAL LETTER WRITTEN BY MAGGIE O'BRIEN

To the Secretary Air Minister, London, England   1925

Sir,
I am writing to inquire if Luit Pat Alva O'Brian of the Royal Flying corps ever received his discharge papers. I his Mother am inquiring, my son is now dead, I have never been able to find them in his belongings. I also would like to know if he has pay coming to him.

I wrote to Ottawa Canada and they referred me to you. As you can see by the enclosed letter. Hoping to hear from you soon. I remaining yours respectfully,

Mrs. Margaret O'Brien, Momence, Illinois, U.S.A.

January 4, 1930

Ten years after Pat's death, Margaret received a letter that surely must have been heartbreaking and heartwarming at the same time. It came from the young man whose father welcomed Pat into their home less than fifteen minutes after Pat successfully crawled to freedom under an electrified fence at the Holland border. Now a cleric, the young man did not know Pat was dead.

MOTHER OF WORLD WAR HERO RECEIVES LETTER FROM HOLLAND

A FRIEND OF LIEUTENANT PAT O'BRIEN WRITES, UNAWARE OF HIS DEATH.

On Saturday, Jan. 4th, 1930, Mrs. Margaret O'Brien received a letter written to her son, Pat O'Brien, the writer not knowing that Pat had been dead for several years.

The missive came from far away Holland and the writer was a friend who sheltered Pat in his home the first night after his escape from the Germans by leaping from a moving train while being transferred from one German prison camp to another during the world war.

Following is the letter:

Nijmegen, Holland.
December 21st.

My Dear Mr. Pat O'Brien:

In the first place many thanks for your kind lines and your photo which you sent me once. Do you remember it? I must ask you to kindly excuse my tardy reply. Do you remember me? It is now about thirteen years ago since I met you near the Belgian frontier in the village of Maarheese—that night you stayed with us and the next day I accompanied you toward Eindhoven, there we said "goodbye."

Afterwards I received your letter in which you told me your vicissitudes.

Where have you been? Some months ago I read in the paper that a Mr. Pat O'Brien set up a new record with the flying machine. Are you this Mr. O'Brien? In that case my cordial congratulations on your success.

You should do me a great pleasure to write me once. Meanwhile, I have become religious and I am doing very well. With kindly regards,

Yours Affectionately,
Brother Venansius.

Anson C. uns
Graafrcheweg 274
Nijmegen, Holland.

October 9, 1930

Momence Press Reporter

DEATH CALLS MOTHER OF WORLD WAR HERO
Mrs. Margaret O'Brien Dies on Wednesday
Funeral To Be Held at Methodist Church
On Saturday Afternoon at 2:00 O'clock

Mrs. Margaret O'Brien, one of Momence's best known and most beloved women, died at her home in this city about 3:00 Wednesday afternoon, after an illness of several months. While it was known that her condition was serious, none were prepared to hear of her passing away. For some time Mrs. O'Brien had been afflicted with heart trouble which some time ago developed into dropsy, since which time she had been gradually growing weaker. She was able to be about her home most every day until Wednesday, when she grew suddenly worse, and soon sank into unconsciousness from which she did not revive.

In 1872 she came to Momence with her parents and the same year was united in marriage to Mr. Daniel O'Brien and to this union nine children were born, five of whom survive, Perry of Gary, Ind., Ivan, Clarence and Mrs. Clara Clegg of this city and Merwin of Los Angeles, California. Her husband died on December 7, 1901, and she was left with a family of children, but her determination to hold the family together was successful, although it meant great sacrifice on her part. Her motherly love was sufficient to surmount all obstacles, and the tender and loving care which she gave has always been the admiration of all who knew her.

During the World War she had the pleasure of seeing her son, Pat O'Brien, gain world fame and honor, in his heroic war record, and especially by his escape from a German prison, which was one of the outstanding heroic achievements of the war. During the few years following her son's return from France she had many honors showered upon her which were brought to a sad end in Pat's tragic death. In sadness or joy, in prosperity or adversity, she was ever the same lovable character and her entire life was one which won the love and esteem of everyone.

In early youth she joined the Christian church, but after coming to Momence she affiliated with the Methodist church, and has given many years of loving and faithful service to the church here. She was never known to utter an unkind word to anyone, and the devotion which she gave to her nine fatherless children will ever be remembered by the people of this community.

She was the last surviving member of the local Rebekah lodge, and was also a member of the W. R. C. and in both of these organizations she gave real and valuable service. She was ever ready to assist in every worthy cause and patriotic service and she will be sadly missed in this community. The funeral services will be held on Saturday afternoon at 2:00 o'clock from the Methodist church with the pastor Rev. Smith officiating. The services at the grave will be under the auspices of the Rebekahs and the Past Presidents of Woman's Relief Corps will act as honorary pallbearers. The interment will be in the family lot at the Momence Cemetery.

MARGARET "MAGGIE" O'BRIEN & PAT THE DAY HE CAME HOME FROM WAR

In Pat's own words

One of the few records of Pat's personal reflection on how war changed his view of life

THE
GOSPEL IN THE LIGHT OF
THE GREAT WAR

By

OZORA S. DAVIS

Among the men whose experiences have been fascinating by virtue of their daring and endurance is Lieutenant Pat O'Brien. In an article from his pen occurs the following bit of interesting testimony:

People ask me what I have got out of the war; what, if anything, I have gained from all the experiences I went through. I hadn't analyzed it at first, but now I think I know. All of us who have been over there have come back with a more serious outlook on life than we used to have. I was what I suppose you would call an individualist—and I was the individual! I thought chiefly of *my* fun, *my* happiness, *my* pleasures.

But I've learned that life is something more than a happy-go-lucky adventure. Perhaps going through some hardships of my own has made me more sensitive to suffering in others. I know what it is to be hungry, to be lonely, to be in physical pain. Seeing men's lives snuffed out in a moment can't help affecting your own attitude toward life and death.

The boys who have been over there have a new feeling about religion, even though they may not talk much about it. I know I see fellows going to church now who, I am certain, never used to go there. Someone asked me the other day if I ever thought of praying when I was in a fight in the air. Yes, I did! It is so instinctive that it seems to me pretty good proof that there is a Supreme Being to whom we naturally turn.

THE UNIVERSITY OF CHICAGO PRESS
CHICAGO, ILLINOIS

In Ozora S. Davis' book, "The Gospel in the Light of the Great War," Pat is quoted, along with other vets about the effect war has had on their view of humanity and life itself.

At right: Methodist Church of Momence where Pat's funeral was held.

The above discribes one of Shakespeer's most charming heroines, but it came into my mind as being a most appropriate heading for an article on our "Pat." As I sat and listened for the 3rd time to the story of his wonderful escape from the Huns. And yet, the story was as fascinating to me as the oft repeated Fairy tales of my childhood. We really never grow up; we are always children in our delight in the heroic and wonderful, and this is as it should be. Always, will a story of adventure and daring grip our hearts and hold our attention. And the story of Pat O'Brien's escape from the huns will be told by our children's children to their children and will be listened to by them with the same keen attention with which we have listened to it.

Pat is so very human; that is why we love him. No hero on a pedestal is he—but a man among men, a boy among boys. In spite of the marvels of courage and daring which he represents, in spite of having made the seeming impossible, posible. He tells us naively as a little child, that it was only through God's help that he was able to keep on, and not give way to despair. He tells us that any of our American boys could have done the same. Thousands have cheered him, the Great of our land and also of England have delighted to show him honor, but he has not lost his head or his feet. He is still firmly planted on the earth and brothers to his kind, a very real Irishman in an American body, with a soul that embraces the world. He is one of those rare characters that while holding love of native land above all, can still see the good and glory of other lands. Can see the good points even in an enemy. His the soul that can fight with all the fierceness of hate and still feel no personal hatred, for his foe.

PAT'S LEGACY...

From someone who heard him speak in Momence

Every moment of his lecture given last Sunday afternoon at the Kankakee Chautauqua was a delight to his hearers. He was cheered again and again; and his regret at not being able to stand on his head, so that a lady in the rear might have a good view of his wonderful Holland shoes, brought down the house.

When he told of his conversation with the King of England, in which he informed his majesty, that the only part of a carrot he really liked was the green tops; he made a lasting friend of every man, woman and child in the audience who had a drop of Irish blood in their veins.

A valuable tip was given to the farmers, when he told of how the Belgians backed up the rear end of the family cow into the kitchen during the winter, to keep the milk from freezing. Little things like these kept the audience in good humor in spite of the intense heat. But it was when he told of his escape, of how he had crawled under the live wire and emerged safely on the Holland side, and realized that once more he was free. When he told of how he had fallen on his knees and thanked the All Father for His loving watch and care, through all his trials. It was then, that the real Pat O'Brien was revealed. Our Pat! America's Pat! God's Pat. The one that gave to us the splendid motto that will help timid souls over the hard places of life. "It is foolish ever to despair."

There were many things written about Pat. On occasion the more thoughtful journalist, seeing the fantastic in Pat O'Brien would recognize him as the exception. This article from the Philadelphia Ledger speaks to Pat's special nature. It might surprise the reader to read the reference to Pat's race and the common belief at the time that the Irish took risks.

PAT O'BRIEN: HE'S ALL RIGHT

It goes without saying that the American aviator who was hit by a bullet, fell 8,000 feet, and after recovering in a hospital, jumped from a train in order to escape a German prison camp, rejoices in the name of Patrick Alva O'Brien, of Momence, Ill., says the Philadelphia Ledger. One does not have to go back to Lever or Dumas to know that there are venturesome souls in this world who compel their fate by being indifferent to it. They take their life in their hands and it is because of this that they save it. With all the inconsequence of a race whose every anecdote turns quaintly on the actually impossible, Pat O'Brien took his chances in the British flying corps, but never let his chances take him. He thought they "had him", or, as the phrase goes, "he had got his'n" when he was hit in midair, but that was an allowable error of judgment natural under the somewhat exciting and disconcerting circumstances. Nor was his time up when he jumped the train going thirty-five miles an hour well inside the German lines. And so once more a youthful and debonair Sir Lucius O'Trigger makes a world somewhat weary of doctrinaires who would ignore racial and individual heredity and improve it by mere verbal say so, his debtor.

There is something in temperament after all, and despite all the prudent copy-book rules as to the danger that lies in foolhardiness there are always the rash who succeed by their magnificent audacity. If in some cases the type is Latin as in the familiar "Here I am, here I remain" of the hero of the Malakoff, it is oftener Celtic and Celtic even when disguised under foreign names. Indeed, the enthusiastic Irish who can prove to you that all the great battles of the world have been won by Irishmen have something back of their fantasy. For the Pat O'Briens are typical of their race and its heroes; they not only do not hesitate to rush in where angels fear to tread—they do, and carry the angels along with them; for, of course, it was a soldier from the Emerald Isle that Shakespeare was thinking of when he described him as "seeking the bubble reputation even in the cannon's mouth." But remember, to your Pat O'Briens it is the cannon's mouth that they are after, not the bubble reputation. That is always secondary, but they get it just the same.

THE TOWN THAT WOULD NOT FORGET
by Kevin McNulty, Sr.

As long as I can remember, I knew the name Pat O'Brien. As a young kid, I heard his name mentioned but like all eight-year-olds in the fifties, Pat O'Brien might as well have been Hopalong Cassidy to me. Eventually, in my teen years, I learned he was a real person, a war hero, someone who was very famous and someone that, it was said, killed himself. Every time I heard the phrase "killed himself," it was always following by "but the family never believed he did it."

There are and always have been a lot of "characters" in Momence, some were famous and a good number infamous. But there was a generation ten to twenty years older than me that knew more about Pat. The tale of Pat O'Brien was told many times over by the "older folks" and weaved its way into the fabric of Momence history.

I was fortunate to live next door Pierre and Elaine Saindon. Elaine was an O'Brien, a descendant of Pat's brother. I met the O'Briens of my time and was in the same class as Colleen O'Brien, daughter of Jack O'Brien. I learned a bit more about Pat, enough to know he was real, and that there was an unresolved mystery surrounding his death. In addition, although Rex Rowe was the Mayor of Momence as long as I could remember, I knew nothing of Rex's bravery, war service and time as a World War Two POW. When I left Momence in 1970, that was the extent of my knowledge of these two men.

The next time I encountered the name Pat O'Brien was in 2007 when I received a call from Marcia Tedford, a long time Momence resident who I recalled having a bunch of kids around her when I was a teen. She's a feisty woman who most would say is someone you can go to if you "want to get something done." Marcia had assisted Rex Rowe in finding the records of Pat O'Brien. I learned through Marcia how revered Rex was to the World War Two generation. When I studied his war record, I understood why he was mayor all those years. He was shot on the Normandy Beach and spent the rest of the war in a German POW camp.

The U.S. Military records, including all of Pat's were lost in a fire in St. Louis. Rex Rowe died with no proof of Pat's service to the U.S. military. But a marker was acquired through donations solicited by Rex and a dedication was held on July, 31, 2007. I was not there.

Following the event, Marcia asked me to meet her in her office one day. I had published a small book about Momence in 2007. She asked me if I would "write the story of Pat O'Brien." I hadn't received a gift that great since my dad gave me my first bicycle.

Above: Pat's grave marked in 2007. Tall stone behind his grave is that of his father Daniel O'Brien

Below: Momence Honor Guard - 21 Gun Salute 2007

Memorial Dedication
Lieutenant Patrick Alva O'Brien
December 13, 1890 - December 20, 1920

Tuesday, July 31, 2007
11:30 a.m.
Momence Cemetery
Momence, Illinois

Lieutenant Patrick Alva O'Brien

Memorial Dedication

Opening Prayers	Reverend Michael Frazier Calvary Baptist Church Momence, Illinois
"Amazing Grace" Bagpipes	Mary Bock Steger, Illinois
Introduction	Mr. Bill Cotter, Director Momence Honor Guard Momence, Illinois
Presentation of British Flag	Honorable Andrew Seaton Consul- General British Consulate Chicago, Illinois
Comments	Mr. Rex Rowe Momence, Illinois
Flyover	Dr. Brian Olofsson Kankakee, Illinois

Patrick Alva O'Brien

Pat has been a special interest of mine, not just because he served with 66 squadron, but because of his varied life. When I first came across him he was a pilot, then he was an escapee in the most dramatic of circumstances, he showed how tenacious he was with his march across Germany to safety in Holland, and then he became a Hollywood movie star. I am delighted and humbled to find that there are still many people who after nine decades are still appreciative of what the men who fought WWI went through and that one remarkable forgotten Airman has again found honour in his community with the marking of his last place of rest.

John Grech - Surrey, England
www.66squadron.co.uk

Patrick O'Brien Timeline

1890	December 13 - Date of Birth
1912	Began flying career, Chicago
1914	Began working the Santa Fe Railroad
1916	Arrived in Canada, joined the Royal Flying Corps
1917	May-Left for England with 17 other candidates
	June-Receives Royal Aero Club Certificate 5397
	July-Posted to 66 Squadron via Pilots Pool, France
	August-Pat's plane downed, wounded, and captured by Germans
	September-Pat dives through train window to escape imprisonment
	November-Pat reaches Dutch borders and freedom
	November-Returns to England and cables "Mom" "I'm OK"
	December-England's King George V requests Pat's presence
1918	January-Momence Welcomes Home It's Hero
	March-"Outwitting the Hun" is published - best seller
	March-resigns his RFC commission
	Tours the US promoting book and raising money for War Relief
	Travels to China, Japan, and Gobie Desert
1919	December-King George V awards Pat the Military Cross
1920	January-marries Virginia Allen in Cuba
	June-partners with S.A. Hedding in auto dealership
	Make movie, "Shadows of the West" with Virginia Allen, released in 1921
	December 17-tragically ends his own life

Members of the O'Brien family and Momence residents attend Memorial. Below Jack O'Brien, then receives flag from Brittish Counsel

THE TRUNK

For years Pat's travel trunk was stored in the attic of his best friend Al Fountaine. In 2007, is was discovered and given to a member of the family in Momence where it is today.

Francis and Diane Fountaine, son and daughter of Pat's best friend Al Fountaine show where truck was.

Carol (O'Brien) Hughes Floto

Carol ~ Three years into the writing of "Lt. Pat O'Brien," we received a phone call from a woman in Reno, Nevada. Her name was Leslie Floto. Leslie, and her sister Lori, had been on-line looking for more information on Pat O'Brien. Their father Kenneth Bernard Floto had passed away approximately six years previous. Their mother, Carol had died earlier. Both had full lives and Floto had a highly decorated military career.

Kevin McNulty received the call from Leslie Floto and will never forget the first words spoken by Leslie.

"Are you the guy writing the story of Pat O'Brien," she asked?

To which McNulty responded, "Yes."

Then Leslie said, "Well, I am the illegitimate granddaughter of Pat O'Brien."

That phone call opened up a chapter in Pat O'Brien's life that the authors had no knowledge of, citizens of Momence never spoke of, and the O'Brien family itself never knew of. Pat O'Brien had been a father and no one knew.

But who was the mother?

All that Momence knew was that Pat worked in California before he joined the service. What no one but the Flotos knew was the romance between Pat O'Brien and their blood-grandmother Agnes MacMillan.

Carol (O'Brien) Hughes Floto was the daughter of Agnes MacMillan and Pat O'Brien. Their story changed everything and when the Flotos found us we felt we had finally found the real Pat O'Brien.

FLOTO FAMLY TREE

Pat O'Brien - Agnes MacMillan

Carol Ruth
(Caroline)

George & Vesta Hughes
(Raised Carol her whole life)
No other children

****

Kenneth Bernard Floto .... Carol Ruth Hughes

Children

Leslie	Jon	Lori
Donald Jacobs	Married Agnes Volk	Not Married

Children

Christine and Meredith Hanolsy
    Nickolas
    Zachary

Jeremy & Cassadra Jacobs
    Luella
    Orla

Robert & Bethany Jacobs

    Grady
    Campbell

George Hughes, Vesta Hughes and Carol (O'Brien) Hughes

An arrangement was made between Agnes MacMillan and Hughes' that they would raise Carol. Agnes would be able to visit and was referred to as "Aunt Agnes." According the Leslie and Lori, it came a point in Carol's late teens where she resisted Agnes not wanting her to visit as much. It was one thing to receive presents every holiday and every birthday from Aunt Agnes but once she hit eighteen or nineteen years old she wanted to see Agnes less. "She was torn," according the Lori. . "She loved her parents. Why did she have to have this other women in her life?" she said.

Carol was never told that Agnes was her mother but, according to Leslie, Carol told them later in life that she "figured it out on my own" at about age 13. Agnes was more motherly with Carol than Vesta.

WEDDING DAY
Carol and Ken Floto married during the war (WWII)

Ken Floto was a career military officer. He was an Army Colonel with the Infrantry. His family was well-to-do having a grandfather who sold nearly all coal to early San Francisco residents. Ken, like Pat, was bored with school. He was sent to a boarding school in Portland after quitting high school out of boredom. He was a highly organized man, quite daring and had the ability to make quick decisions which served him well as he rose in the ranks of the Army. How interesting that Pat O'Brien's daughter would marry a gentleman similar to him. Quick decision making and daring personality certainly describes Pat.

As a result of his military career the Flotos (and their children) lived all over the world. When Kevin McNulty asked Lori Floto where they were from she answered, "all over the world." They did, in fact, see the world.

Carol joined Special Services after high school. Her role took her to Alaska for her first assignment. Without telling the Hugh's she and her friends took a bike ride from San Francisco to Alaska to 'take a look at her new job location." One cannot help but think of the comparisons to many of Pat's exploits before he left for service. Carol met Ken in the service while they were both stationed in Europe following V-E Day.

CAROL IN PARIS V-J DAY

Carol arrived in Paris, France on V-J. It was the end of the war. She served with Special Services, helping the GI's get re-acclimated to civilian life. Once the NAZIs were defeated in Europe, the gals were sent over.

She told the story to her girls:

"My girlfriend and I were walking to work, just two of us, and word had just hit the streets that the Japanese had surrendered. GI's were dancing all over the streets of Paris.

These GI's were posing for a picture and one guy yelled, 'Hey Red!" come join us!"

Carol is dead-center in the middle in this photo.

CAROL TAKES ACTION

Carol told her daughters the following about their dad:

"When I first saw your father over in Europe I said to my girlfriend,

'I better get that guy right away before someone else grabs him!'

I coudn't figure out why the guy wasn't married yet."

FLOTO FAMILY
Ken Floto, Leslie (standing), Lori, Jon & Carol
LORI & LESLIE today

THE FLOTOS IN RETIREMENT YEARS

The Flotos had a good life in the service our country. Ken was an infantry soldier who was severely injured twice. In the childrearing years they traveled with their kids, giving them experiences few kids have.

Author McNulty with Lori Floto and Leslie Jacobs in Reno - 2014

When you write a story about a real person that lived well before your time, you live back in that time. A Novel like "Lt. Pat O'Brien" requires one read at least ten-times the material you write not only acquire facts but understand the times, conditions and, most importantly, the people you are writing about.

Meeting the children of Al Fountain and the Flotos in Nevada made the story of Pat O'Brien very real and very close to the current day. Writers will tell you that they feel as though they lose a family member when a book the scope of "Lt. Pat O'Brien" is finished. I will also tell you that there are also moments of emotion experienced for Pat, his family and my home town of Momence as I read the newspaper stories of the joys and sorrows of Pat's life.

Meeting the Flotos made Pat bigger. The life of Ken and Carol is a story in itself. While we still have not seen pictures of Agnes, there's a good chance we will. More stories will be told.

THE RETURN OF PAT O'BRIEN
(One of the many Poems written about Pat by admirers)
1918

"My great big boy!" "My great big boy!"
the mother cried, with pride and joy
Once more he held her in his arm-
The boy just back from war's alarm

Back with honor for had he not
Withstood the fire of shell and shot
Flew o'er the "Huns" and gave the hell
And victory won with shell for shell

High in the heavens they reached their aim
And down to earth fell our hero game
 into the hands of the cruel foe.
But not for long, thank God we know.

No prisoner he - he jumped the train
Once more on earth and free again
Returns to the land that gave him birth

The town runs out to greet her boy
The bands burst forth with welcome joy
Men, women, boys and all were crying
God bless the name of pat O'Brien

Of all his triumphs that was the best
Back to his home to the mother next
The look that he saw within her eyes
Was more to him than fame or prize

Such are the men America sends
To fight for liberty, homes and friends
The Stars and the Stripes above the fly
They'll dare, they do, they'll conquer, not die.

OTHER BOOKS BY KEVIN MCNULTY, SR.

"Around Momence" by Kevin McNulty, Sr.
Copyright © 2007 Kevin McNulty, Sr.
Published by Arcadia Publishing
Charleston SC, Chicago IL, Portsmouth NH, San Francisco, CA
ISBN 978-07358-57289

"Lt. Pat O'Brien" by Kevin McNulty, Sr.
Copyright © 2013 KMC PUBLISHING COMPANY
All rights reserved.
ISBN: 10-0615852114
ISBN-13: 978-0615852119

"Outwitting the Hun" by Lt. Pat O'Brien.
Originally written and published in 1918 ~ Republished 2013
Copyright © 2013 KMC PUBLISHING COMPANY
Reprint includes added details and notes written by Kevin McNulty, Sr. that Pat was unable to write in the first print during the war years.
ISBN- 978-0-9897965-0-7

"The Barns of Kankakee County" by Kevin McNulty, Sr.
Copyright © 2014 KMC PUBLISHING COMPANY
All Photography is property of Kevin McNulty, Sr.
ISBN-10: 0989796515
ISBN-13: 978-0-9897965-1-4

Marcia Tedford & Kevin McNulty

Kevin McNulty, Sr. grew up in Momence, Illinois, located in Kankakee County. He is a local historian, author, musician, composer, amateur photographer and has a twenty-six-year career in business.

He began his career as a high school music teacher for fifteen years. He then spent twenty-six years leading trade associations and lobbying for business He has extensive experience in China helping American companies sell to the Chinese and invest in China domestic projects. He returned to music teaching in 2012 and is currently the Orchestra Director, Assistant Director of Bands at Bradley-Bourbonnais Community High School in Bradley, Illinois.

He is author of four books including the 800-page historical novel *"Lt. Pat O'Brien"*(2013), about the famous American pilot who flew for the British during World War I. McNulty is the author of *"Around Momence"* (2007), published by Arcadia Publishing, and *"Barns of Kankakee County"* (2013), published by his publishing company KMC Publishing Company based in Matteson, Illinois. KMC Publishing has also re-published *"Outwitting the Hun"* (1918/2014) written by Pat O'Brien about his escape from German hands in World War

McNulty's publications are available on Amazon and eBay or directly from his publishing company: KMC Publishing Company, P.O. Box 1505, Matteson, IL 60443, 708-747-9182 or kevin@kmcglobalonline.com

Marcia Tedford is a long-time resident of Momence. She has been active in many local community organizations including the Momence Chamber of Commerce, and many others. Her husband was the owner Tedford Motors in Momence and Kankakee, Illinois. Marcia currently manages the office of Momence Township in Momence.

www.ingramcontent.com/pod-product-compliance
Lightning Source LLC
Chambersburg PA
CBHW081222170426
43198CB00017B/2686